A KID'S GUIDE TO
CHESS

LEARN THE GAME'S RULES, STRATEGIES, GAMBITS, AND THE MOST POPULAR MOVES TO BEAT ANYONE!

Ellisiv Reppen
Illustrated by Flu Hartberg

Sky Pony Press
NEW YORK

Sky Pony Press books may be purchased in bulk at special discounts for sales promotion, corporate gifts, fund-raising, or educational purposes. Special editions can also be created to specifications. For details, contact the Special Sales Department, Sky Pony Press, 307 West 36th Street, 11th Floor, New York, NY 10018 or info@skyhorsepublishing.com.

Sky Pony® is a registered trademark of Skyhorse Publishing, Inc.®, a Delaware corporation. Visit our website at www.skyponypress.com.

10 9 8 7 6 5

Library of Congress Cataloging-in-Publication Data is available on file.

Cover design by Kai Texel
Cover illustration credit: Flu Hartberg

Print ISBN: 978-1-5107-6652-5
Ebook ISBN: 978-1-5107-6692-1

Printed in China

Portions of this book were previously published as *Chess* (ISBN: 978-1-63450-160-6).

Contents

Preface

Are you ready to become a master of chess?

Chess is played on all continents and by millions of people. It is the world's most popular board game, and is enjoyed by people of all ages.

In this book you will get to know the movements of the different pieces, and how you should play in the different phases of the game. Whether you never have touched a chess piece before, or you already have some experience, you can learn something from this book.

You will get exclusive advice from some of the world's best chess players. These brilliant tips will help you become a pro at chess. Imagine the joy of winning a game of chess against a classmate, or even your grandfather!

In addition, you will have the opportunity to try and solve problems that world champions have created.

If you have a chessboard, you should use it while reading, although it is not imperative.

Get ready to concentrate; it is time for your brain to do some exercise!

Rules of the Game and Its Battlefield

Chess is a board game where two opponents play against each other in what we call a chess game. One player controls the white pieces, the other controls the black pieces.

Whoever controls the white pieces always makes the first move of the game. The players then alternate moves. Each time a player moves one of their chess pieces, we call it a move.

Chess is a game where you act as a general and try to lead your army of chess pieces in a smarter way than your opponent.

The chess pieces move in different ways, and you're allowed to capture your opponent's pieces. The goal of the game is to checkmate the opponent's king. Whoever manages to do this first has won.

The chessboard represents the battlefield of the game. It is divided into 64 squares, half of them black and half of them white.

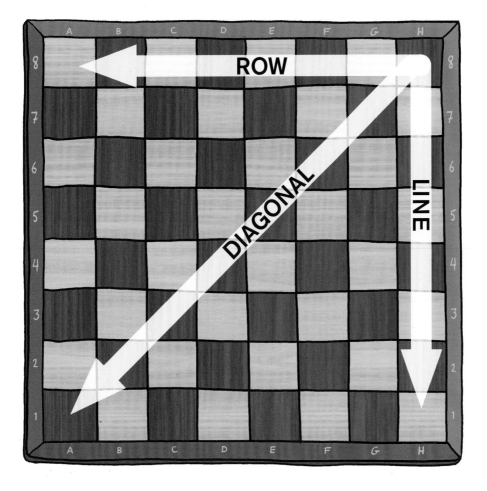

The chessboard consists of rows, lines, and diagonals.

Each player has a king, a queen, two rooks, two bishops, two knights, and eight pawns.

King **Queen** **Rook** **Bishop** **Knight** **Pawn**

This is how the pieces are set up at the start of the game. A good way to memorize the setup is to remember that the white pieces are placed on rows number one and two, and the black pieces on rows number seven and eight. The white queen is always placed on a white square in the beginning, and the black queen on a black square.

Did you know that chess was originally a game of war? The old Indian name for the game was *Tschaturanga*, which means *army*.

Did you know that the painting of a chessboard is called a diagram? You will see several types of chessboard diagrams in this book.

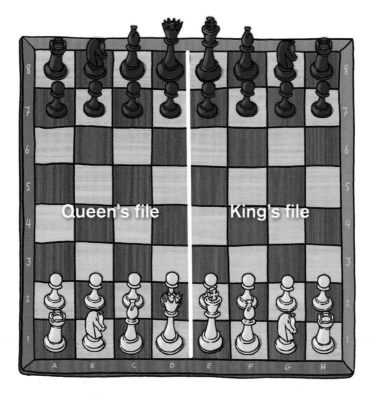

The chessboard is divided into the king's file and queen's file. At the start of the game, all of the pieces on the king's side belong to the king's file, and the pieces on the queen's side belong to the queen's file.

Did you pay attention? Test yourself and see if you can pass the chess test on the next page.

CHESS CHECK 1

How many squares are there on a chessboard?

A) 8

B) 64

C) 100

CHESS CHECK 2

Who starts the game?

A) White

B) Black

C) A coin toss decides

CHESS CHECK 3

Which pieces should you start with?

A) A king, a queen, two rooks, two bishops, two knights, and eight pawns

B) Three kings, four queens, and twelve pawns

C) Nine queens and one king

CHESS CHECK 4

What colors are there on a traditional chessboard?

A) Black and white

B) Yellow and blue

C) Green and red

CHESS CHECK 5

Which row do the white pawns start on?

A) Row 1

B) Row 2

C) Row 7

(Answer Key p. 167)

How the Pieces Move

The pieces move in different ways, but all of them can capture their opponent's pieces. You can never capture your own pieces. When you make a capture, you move one of your own pieces to a square where your opponent has a piece. You have now captured your opponent's piece, and the square is yours.

The Rook

The rook can be moved as far as you want, forward, backward, and sideways. It cannot jump over any of the other pieces, your own or those of your opponent.

Did you know that the rook has the option of moving to fourteen different squares on an open chessboard, no matter where on the board it is located? Try it out yourself!

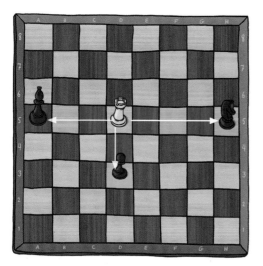

The rook captures other pieces in the same way as it moves.

The English word *rook* derives from the Persian word *rukh*, which means *wagon*. The rook can move fast and far, but not diagonally and not if there are any pieces blocking its way, just like a wagon.

The Bishop

The bishop can be moved as far as you want, but only diagonally. Both players have two bishops each, one that can move along the white squares and one that can move along the black squares. The bishop cannot jump over any of the other pieces, your own or those of your opponent.

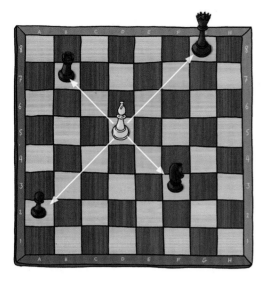

The bishop captures other pieces in the same way as it moves.

Did you know that originally, bishops were called *elephants*? Still today, the name is alive in several languages. In Russia they call the bishop *slon*, which is the Russian word for elephant.

The Queen

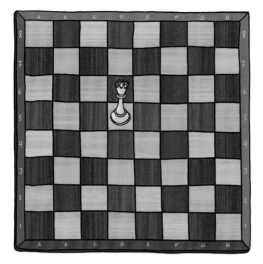

The queen can move as far as she wants forward, backward, to the sides, and diagonally. The queen cannot jump over any of her own, or her opponent's, pieces.

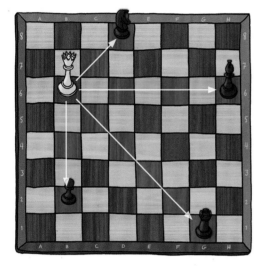

The queen captures other pieces in the same way as she moves.

When the queen is placed on a square in the middle of an open board, there are 27 squares that she can move to. That's nearly half of the chessboard!

The queen is the most powerful piece.

The Knight

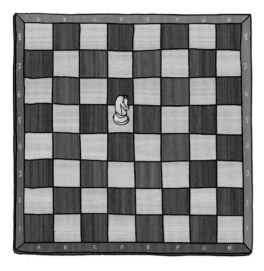

The knight, also known as the horse, moves two squares forward and one to the side, or two squares backward and one to the side.

The knight captures other pieces in the same way as it moves.

The knight represents a soldier.

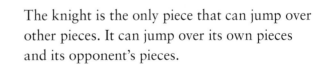

The knight is the only piece that can jump over other pieces. It can jump over its own pieces and its opponent's pieces.

Did you know that a knight that starts on a black square always ends up on a white square? A knight that starts on a white square will always end up on a black square. Try and see for yourself!

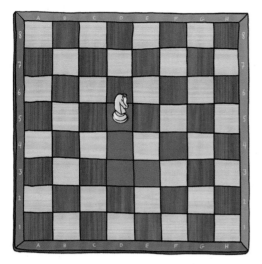

The knight moves like the letter L.

The Pawn

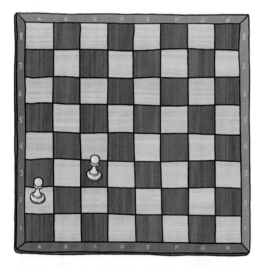

The pawn only moves forward, never backward. The first time a pawn moves, it can move one or two squares. But after the first move, it can only move one square at a time.

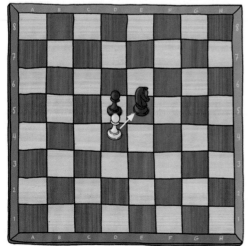

All of the pieces can capture the opponent's pieces in the same way as they move, except for the pawn. The pawn can only capture other pieces that are placed diagonally, one square ahead.

Promotion

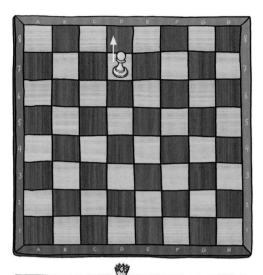

If a pawn advances all the way to the last row of the board, it can be promoted to another piece. The player may choose whether they want their piece to be promoted to a queen, rook, bishop, or knight of the same color.

When a pawn reaches the end of a file and a promotion takes place, the file is also known as the eighth rank.

The promoted piece remains in the same square the promotion took place.

And just like that, the pawn turns into a queen.

The pawns are the foot soldiers of the two armies.

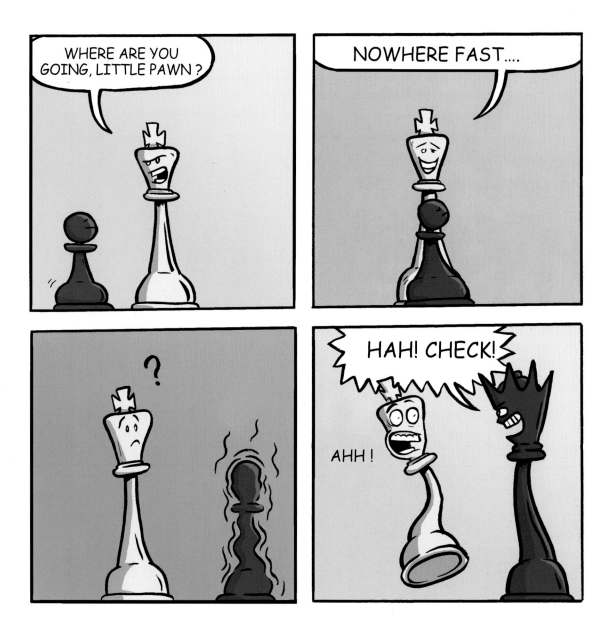

Did you know that you can have nine queens in one game? You can make this happen if you manage to get all of your pawns to the eighth row and promote them to queens.

The King

The king can move forward, backward, sideways, and diagonally, but only one step at the time.

The king captures other pieces in the same way as it moves.

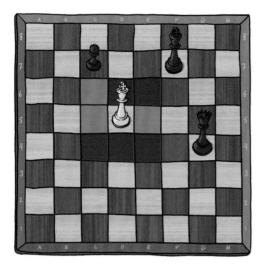

The king is the most important piece in the game.

The king is not allowed to move to a square that is under threat by the opponent's pieces.

The white king can move to the green squares, but is not allowed on the red squares because these are under threat by the black pieces.

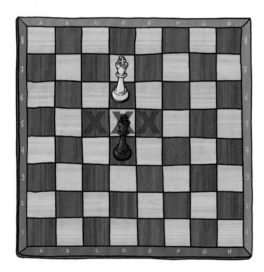

The two kings in the game are not allowed to stand next to each other. There has to be at least one square separating them. So a king piece cannot capture its opponent's king.

The kings cannot move to the squares covered with the red crosses.

Did you know that it is against the rules of chess to move the king to a square where he will be in danger? A player that has done such a move will be forced to withdraw the move and move the king to a square where he will be safe.

Now you have gotten to know the different pieces and learned how they move. If you have a chessboard, you may want to practice by moving the different pieces around. You can challenge your mom, dad, or a friend with a game of chess!

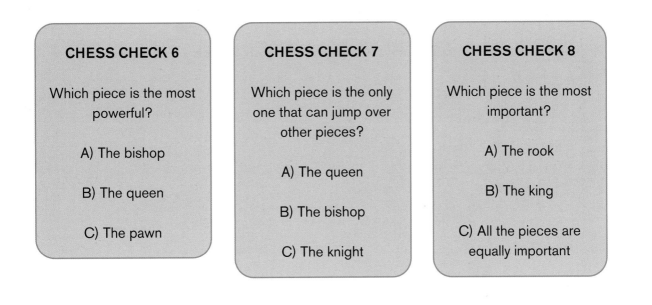

CHESS CHECK 6

Which piece is the most powerful?

A) The bishop

B) The queen

C) The pawn

CHESS CHECK 7

Which piece is the only one that can jump over other pieces?

A) The queen

B) The bishop

C) The knight

CHESS CHECK 8

Which piece is the most important?

A) The rook

B) The king

C) All the pieces are equally important

CHESS CHECK 9

Which piece are there the most of?

A) The bishop

B) The pawn

C) The knight

CHESS CHECK 10

What happens to a pawn when it reaches the last row?

A) It switches color

B) It moves back to the square it started at

C) It is promoted to a different piece

CHESS CHECK 11

Which piece cannot capture the other version of itself?

A) The queen

B) The king

C) All of the pieces can be captured

(Answer Key p. 167)

Standard Chess Phrases

Now that you have stepped into the world of chess, you may want to know a few common terms.

Threaten

The white rook can attack the black knight—it is threatening the black knight. The rook can move to the square where the black knight is and capture the knight.

Cover

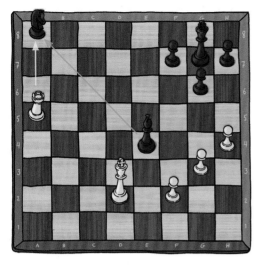

The white rook is threatening the black knight.

The black bishop protects, or covers, the black knight. If the white rook captures the black knight, the black bishop can capture the white rook.

Blunder

A blunder is something you should try to avoid. But it is a lot of fun when your opponent blunders.

Did you know that if you make a mistake on the chessboard it is called a blunder? The black knight just moved to a square where it captured a pawn. This was a huge blunder. The white bishop can now capture the black queen.

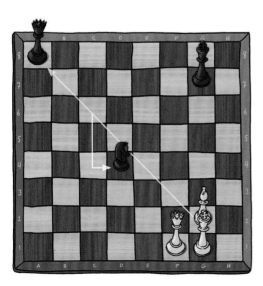

A blunder like this often happens when a player is unfocused. In chess it is essential that the players are fully concentrating during the entire game. You may make a hundred good moves, but if you blunder that hundred and first move, it might lose you the game.

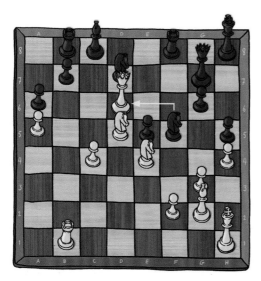

Even the best chess players can blunder if they lose their concentration for just a moment. One of the world's most famous blunders happened by Tigran Petrosjan (World Champion from 1963–1969) during a game against David Bronstein in 1956.

Petrosjan was playing white. Bronstein only had a couple of seconds left in the game. They had played thirty-six moves, and if they played four more, they would be playing on extra time. But Bronstein wouldn't be able to win in those final moves.

Petrosjan's queen was threatened by the black knight. The queen should be moved.

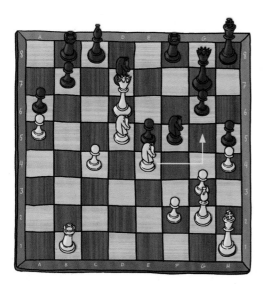

Petrosjan forgot to take the time to analyze his next move and moved his knight instead! Bronstein quickly captured the queen. Petrosjan was so appalled that he immediately gave up. He was so shocked by his mistake that he forgot the shortage of time his opponent was playing on. An incredible double-blunder!

Blunders often decide the outcome of a game. Good advice to avoid blunders is to do the same thing you do before crossing a busy road—look both ways twice. Ask yourself a few questions before you make your move. Why did my opponent make their last move? Are any of my pieces threatened? Is it safe to move my piece to the square that I am considering?

GRANDMASTER TIP

Do not rush into your moves. Try sitting on your hands. This forces you to take a few extra seconds to think before you move. You may find a better move than the one you originally planned to make. Think carefully about before you move—you do not want to blunder!

PIA CRAMLING, SWEDEN

Block

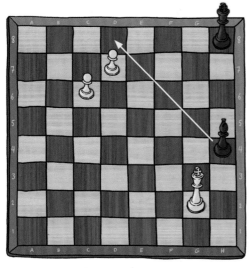

The white pawns have almost reached the other side. The black bishop moves to a square in front of one of the pawns. The pawn can no longer move, and the other pawn is going to be captured by the bishop if it moves. The black bishop is blocking both of the pawns.

Hungry for More Material to read?
If you want to read more books about chess, you may want to visit The Hague in the Netherlands. In the Van der Linde-Niemeijeriana library there are almost 30,000 books about chess!

Chess Olympiad
Chess isn't played in either the Summer or Winter Olympics, but has its very own Chess Olympiad. Approximately 150 countries participate.

CHESS CHECK 12

What does it mean to threaten another chess piece?

A) To attack

B) To capture

C) To make a legal move

CHESS CHECK 13

What does it mean to blunder?

A) To make a mistake

B) To make a smart trick

C) To make an illegal move

CHESS CHECK 14

What does it mean to cover a chess piece?

A) To capture

B) To lose a piece

C) To protect

(Answer Key p. 167)

Castling: A Special Move

Castling is a special move where the king and rook move simultaneously. The king moves two steps toward the rook, and the rook jumps over the king and lands on the square the king just passed. This move will get the king quickly into safety, and the rook gets to play.

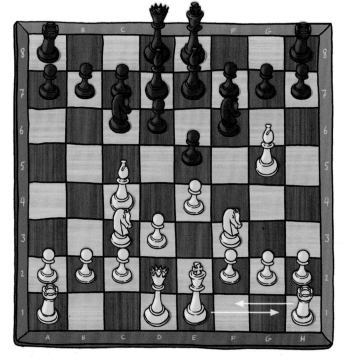

White is castling.

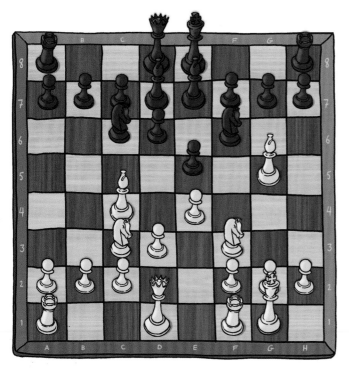

This is how it looks after white has castled. This is called castling short.

Did you know that you always have to move the king first when you castle?

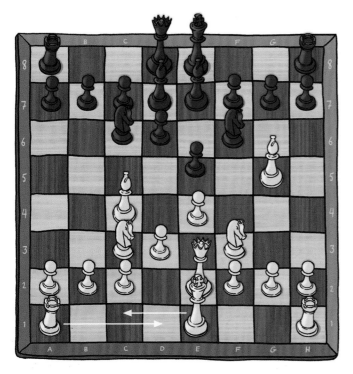

Here, white is castling long.

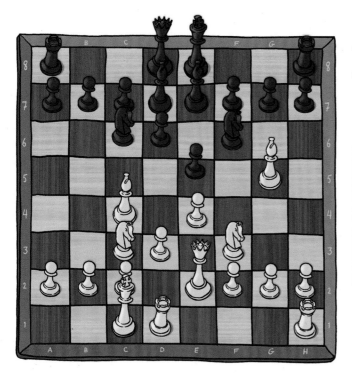

This is how it looks after white has castled long.

Did you know that there are two ways of castling? When the king is castling within his section of the board, he is castling short, and when he is castling within the queen's section, he is castling long.

You cannot castle long if:

- there is one or more pieces standing between your king and your rook
- you have already moved the king or the rook at any time during the game
- the king is in check
- the king has to pass a square where it would be in check
- the king will end up in check

White cannot castle. Do you see why? The king is in check.

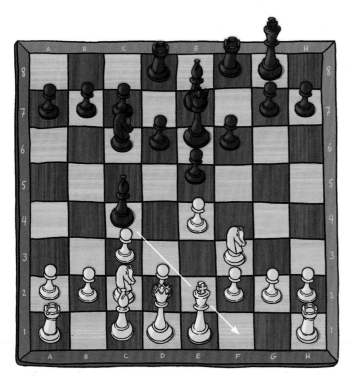

White cannot castle because the king would need to pass a square that is threatened by the black bishop.

Game Clock

A chess timer is used during chess tournaments. It consists of two clocks, one for each player. Both players are playing at a given time. When you have made your move, you press a button on the clock to start your opponent's clock. When your opponent has made their move and pressed the button on their side, your time starts ticking again. If you are out of time before the game is over, you lose. The chess watch counts down and will show 00 when there is no time left.

There are several different types of chess. The most common type is long chess: this is the type that is played in big tournaments, like the world championship. The thinking time varies, but normally a game lasts between three and five hours. Fast chess is a different type of chess. You only have between 15 and 60 minutes to finish the game. The shortest type of chess is called blitz chess. In blitz chess, the players only have a few minutes to finish a game.

In the first chess tournaments, the players did not have any time limits and a game could last for 20 hours. In 1861, the hourglass was introduced as a time controller in a tournament in England. In 1870, the game clock was used for the first time in a tournament in Germany.

White cannot castle because the king would end on a square that is threatened by the black bishop.

White cannot castle long because there is a knight standing between the king and the rook. White cannot castle short either, because the king's rook has already been moved.

Most people need to practice castling a few times before being able to use the move. Even champions have had difficulties remembering how to use this special move during a game. In the 1974 world championship game between Kortsjnoj and Karpov, Kortsjnoj asked a beginner's question: "Am I allowed to castle when my rook is threatened?" The answer is yes.

Don't panic if you find castling difficult. Even professionals who have played in world championships struggle with it.

CHESS CHECK 15

What is castling?

A) A special move where the king moves two steps toward the rook— and the rook jumps over the king

B) A special move where the king and the queen switch places

C) A special move where the rook jumps over the queen

CHESS CHECK 16

How many ways can you castle?

A) One

B) Two—long and short

C) There are no limits

CHESS CHECK 17

When aren't you allowed to castle?

A) If you have moved the queen

B) If you have moved the king or the rook

C) If your opponent has captured one of your pawns

(Answer Key p. 167)

History of Chess

Nobody know for sure where or when chess was invented, but many believe it originated somewhere in Asia before the year 600. Egyptian sculptures have been found that suggest that chess was played in ancient Egypt. It has been assumed that Arabic people brought chess with them to Europe.

Chess has changed over the years, in both the rules and how the pieces move. For instance, castling and the rule that allows pawns to begin by moving two steps were added later on. It is believed that the rules we play by today originated in Spain in the late 15th century.

In the 15th century, the best players were Spanish, but during the 17th century the Italians took over. Chess became very popular in France in the 18th century. And, in the 19th century, the Brits grew to enjoy chess as well. Chess got its own columns in newspapers, and the first international tournament was arranged.

Later, chess continued to spread all around the world. Since World War II, chess has been dominated by Eastern Europeans and former Soviet countries. A few notable players have challenged these champions— among these we have Bobby Fischer from the United States, Viswanathan Anand from India, and Magnus Carlsen from Norway.

The Legend of the Wheat Grain

According to legend, it was the wise Indian man Sissa Ibn Dahir who invented chess because King Sjiram was bored and needed to be entertained. The king became so astonished by the game that he ordered chessboards to be set up in all of his kingdom's temples. He promised the wise man a reward of his own choice.

You may guess that the wise man chose riches—gold, diamonds, or money. But no, instead he chose something very special. He asked for one grain of wheat for the first square on the chessboard, two for the second square, four for the third square, and so on. For each square on the chessboard he would double the number of grains. The king was surprised by his modesty, but ordered for the wise man to get his wish.

The courtiers spent many hours calculating how many grains of wheat the wise man should receive. Eventually, they had to acknowledge that the kingdom did not have enough wheat grains. There were not enough wheat grains in the entire world to meet this demand. The number of wheat grains requested was in fact 18,446,744,073,709,551,615—more wheat grains than were grown on earth. We do not know whether or not the legend is true, but it gives us a hint of the endless possibilities a chessboard offers.

Chess Piece Values

Since all of the pieces move differently, we say that they carry different value depending on how much they can do.

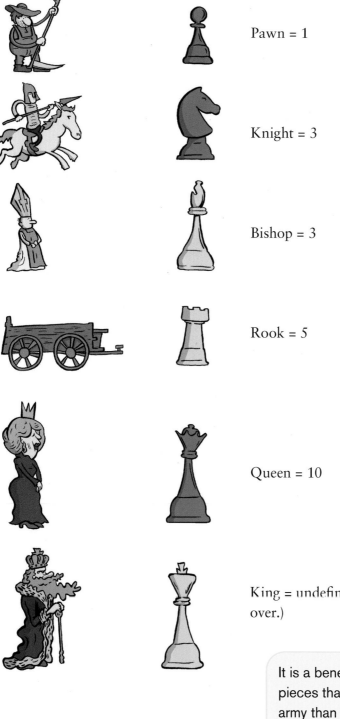

Pawn = 1

Knight = 3

Bishop = 3

Rook = 5

Queen = 10

King = undefined (If the king is captured, game is over.)

It is a benefit to have more and/or better pieces than your opponent. With a bigger army than your opponent, it is easier to attack.

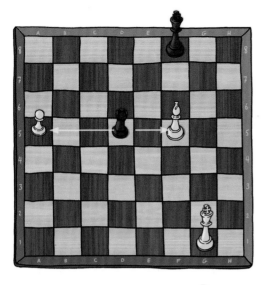

It is smart to pay careful attention to the most valuable pieces.

The black rook is threatening both the white bishop and the white pawn. White can only move one of the pieces. Now the best move is to save the bishop, because the bishop is the most valuable of the two pieces.

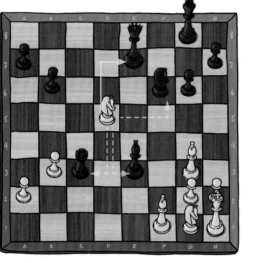

The white knight can capture several of the black pieces. The best move is to capture the queen, because the queen is the most valuable piece.

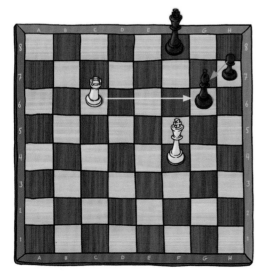

The white rook can capture the black bishop, but that is not a smart move. Why not? Because the bishop is covered by the pawn. If the rook captures the bishop, the pawn will capture the rook in the next move. The rook is worth more than the bishop, therefore it would be a bad trade for the white player.

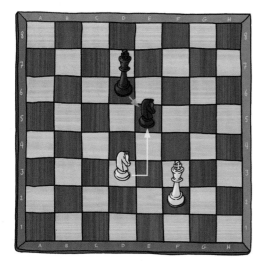

You should avoid trading pieces of more value for less valuable pieces. But trading pieces can be okay if each player gains and loses pieces of equal value.

The white knight captures the black knight, and the black king captures the white knight. Both players have captured pieces worth three points and lost pieces worth three points.

Most often it is better to capture the most valuable piece. Every once in a while some simple arithmetic will help you decide which piece you should capture. Look at this set-up:

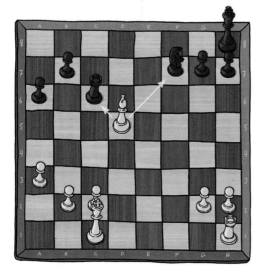

The white bishop is threatening both the black knight and rook. Which is best to choose? If white captures the knight, it will gain three points. Black cannot capture the white bishop in his next move. If white captures the rook, black will capture the white bishop in his next move. White will gain five points, but lose three points. The math tells us 5-3=2 points. Therefore, the smartest move is to capture the knight!

Did you know that in chess the term *material* is used to describe the collected value of the pieces on the board?

Did you know that, theoretically, a chess game can last for 5,949 moves?

The World's Longest Chess Game
The world's longest chess game ever registered was played in Serbia in 1989, between Ivan Nikolic and Goran Arsovic. The game consisted of 269 moves and lasted for 20 hours and 15 minutes! But even then, they could not decide who the winner was. The game ended in a tie.

Good Memory
In 1922, the American champion Frank Marshall played against 155 players simultaneously. Marshall won 126 games, lost 8, and played 21 that ended in ties. The most impressive thing was that after 155 games, he remembered every single move made in 153 of them.

Simultaneous Chess
Simultaneous chess is when one person plays against several people simultaneously. Usually the opponents sit in a row, each with their own board. The person who is playing simultaneously walks from chessboard to chessboard. It is possible to play simultaneously both with and without a chess clock. The person who is playing simultaneously is usually a very strong player.

Checkmate: The Goal of the Game

To win in chess, you are supposed to put your opponent's king in checkmate. This is the goal of the game.

When a king is threatened, we say that he is in check. The king may save himself if he can move, or if the piece that is threatening him can be blocked or captured. If that is impossible, the king is in checkmate, and the game is lost.

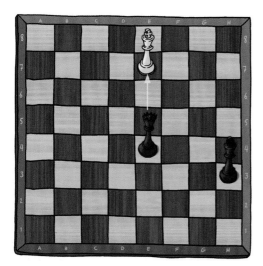

The black queen is threatening the white king. The white king is therefore positioned in check. The king can move and is therefore not in checkmate.

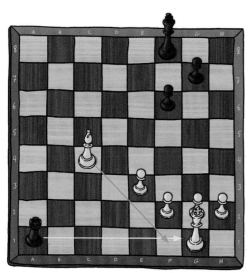

The black rook is threatening the white king. The white king is not allowed to move any places, but it can still be saved. The white bishop can move to the square next to the king.

Do I Have to Say "Check"?
No! If you are threatening your opponent's king, you do not have to say "check." But if your opponent does not see that there is a check and makes another move that does not stop the check, you cannot checkmate the king. You have to tell your opponent, and the move has to be taken back. In tournaments, it is unusual to say "check."

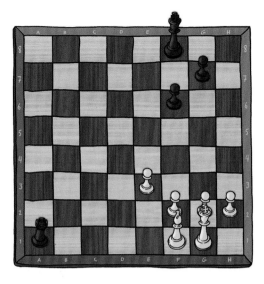

The white bishop is blocking the black rook, and the white king is no longer in check.

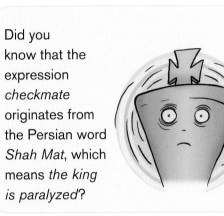

Did you know that the expression *checkmate* originates from the Persian word *Shah Mat*, which means *the king is paralyzed*?

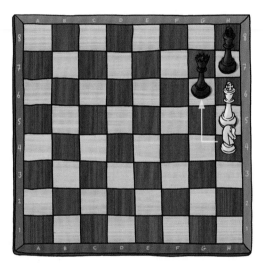

The black queen is threatening the white king. The white king has no legal moves, but is not in checkmate. Do you see why? It is because the white knight can capture the black queen.

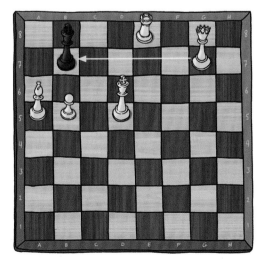

The white queen is threatening the black king, and the other white pieces are threatening all of the other squares surrounding the king. Now the king is placed in checkmate. White has won the game.

All the pieces except the king can place the opponent's king under mate. Since there always must be at least one square between the kings, they can never threaten each other and therefore never checkmate each other.

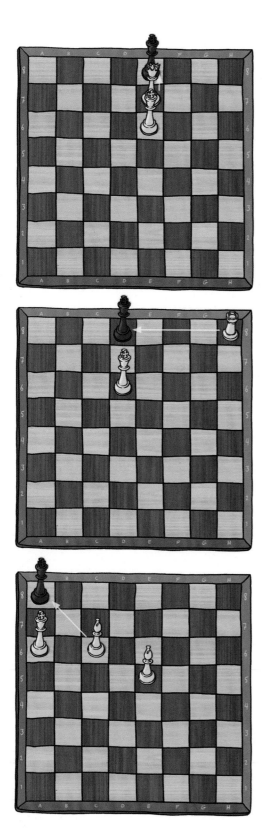

Queen Mate

The white queen has put the black king in checkmate. The black king can therefore not move because the white queen is threatening all the squares surrounding the black king. The black king cannot capture the queen because she is covered by the white king.

Rook Mate

The black king is in checkmate. It cannot move to any of the squares on the eighth row because there are threatened by the rook. The black king cannot move forward because those squares are threatened by the white king.

Bishop Mate

The white bishop has put the black king in checkmate. The black king cannot move because white is threatening all the squares around the king.

Boy: "Grandpa, to you get tired of playing chess?"

Grandpa: "Oh yes. You become exhausted."

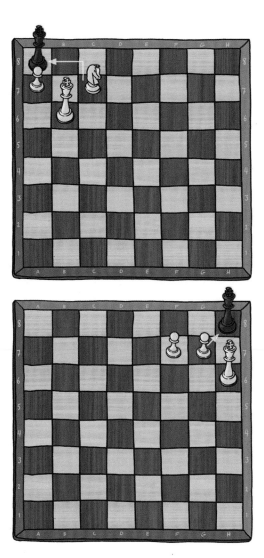

Knight Mate

The white knight has put the king in checkmate. The black king cannot move because the white pieces are threatening all the squares surrounding the king.

Pawn Mate

The pawn placed on the black square has put the king in checkmate. The black king cannot capture the pawn because it is protected by the white king. The black king cannot move to the side because the square is threatened by a pawn standing on white square. The black king cannot move forward because the square is threatened by the white king.

What Is Chess?
Some people say chess is a sport, and the International Olympic Committee (IOC) has recognized chess as such.

There is no doubt that chess a good workout for the brain. Playing chess for hours can be just as physically demanding as playing a soccer match, or any other type of sport. Chess is regarded as a mix of science and mathematics, and many people also consider it an art form.

No matter what you choose to call it, it is without a doubt a very fun game that has brought joy to a lot of people through many centuries, and it will most certainly continue to bring joy to people in the future.

CHESS CHECK 18

What does it mean when
a king is in check?

A) The king is standing
next to a pawn

B) The king is
threatening two pieces

C) The king is threatened

CHESS CHECK 19

How do you win
a chess game?

A) By capturing the king

B) By capturing all your
opponent's pieces

C) By checkmating
the king

CHESS CHECK 20

How many pieces can
place a checkmate?

A) Only the queen

B) The bishops that move
on the white squares

C) All the pieces, except
for the kings

(Answer Key p. 167)

Smart Ways to Checkmate

There are several different ways to checkmate a player. Many mates have their own names. Here are some examples of the most common ways to mate.

Two Rooks Mate

With two rooks, you can create a checkmate (in Norwegian, this particular checkmate is called a *trappematten*, which translates to *stair mate*). To do so, you move the rooks one by one upward like a stair, and you force your opponent's king to one of the corners.

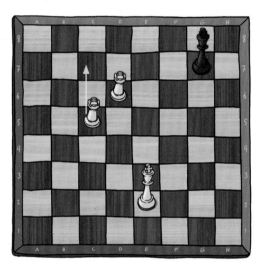

The rook standing in the row furthest away from the black king is moving two rows up.

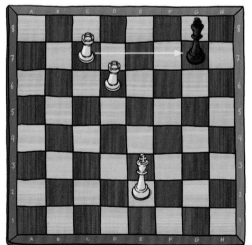

Now the black king is in check and is being pushed one row upward.

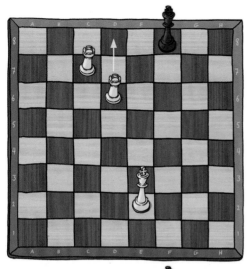

The black king is pushed to the last row, and white can now move the rook in the row furthest away from the king two steps upward.

The black king is in checkmate!

1300   2000   517

Grandmaster

There are several different chess titles, and the highest is grandmaster. Once achieved, the title is held for life. To become a grandmaster, one of the things you have to accomplish is a rating above 2500. The world's youngest grandmaster is the Ukrainian Sergej Karjakin, who achieved the title when he was only twelve years and seven months old. Today there are between 1,000 and 1,500 grandmasters in the world.

Corridor Mate

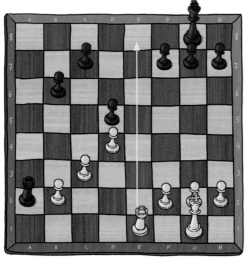

You have a corridor mate (also called a back-rank checkmate) if you have a rook or a queen in the last row and the king is unable to escape because its own pawns are standing in his way. Black just moved its rook and captured a pawn. White can now move its rook to the last row and threaten the black king.

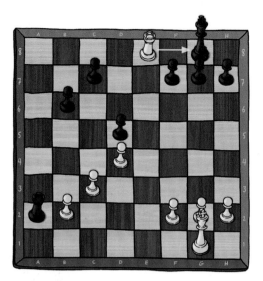

The white rook has put the black king in a corridor mate.

The black pawns are blocking the escape for their own king. This way the king is trapped by his own pieces and the white rook.

GRANDMASTER TIP
To avoid letting your king get trapped, it's smart to make a tiny air hole for your king to breathe. This can be done by moving one of your pawns one square in front of the king.
JAN GUSTAFSSON, GERMANY

Smothered Mate

Smothered mate takes place when a king is trapped, or smothered, by its own pieces and is put in checkmate by a knight.

Did you know that it is impossible to block a knight? When a knight is threatening the opponent's king, it is not legal to place a piece between the knight and the king. If the knight cannot be captured, the king has to move.

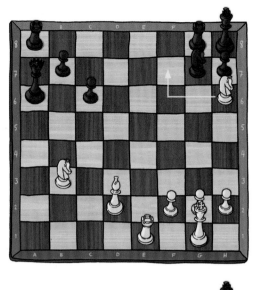

The black king is having trouble breathing in his position in the corner—he is being choked by his own pieces. The white player can exploit this situation. The white knight can move to a square that will threaten the black king.

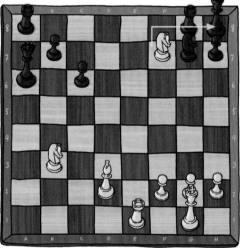

The king is in check, and cannot move. None of the black pieces can capture the white knight. The white knight has put the black king in a smothered mate.

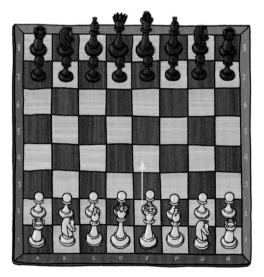

Scholar's Mate

Scholar's mate is a mate that can happen after just four moves.

White starts by moving the pawn in front of the king, two steps forward.

Let's say black moves the pawn in front of the king two steps. White continues by moving the bishop three steps.

Black also decides to move its bishop. White moves its queen four steps.

Black moves the pawn standing in front of the queen, one step.

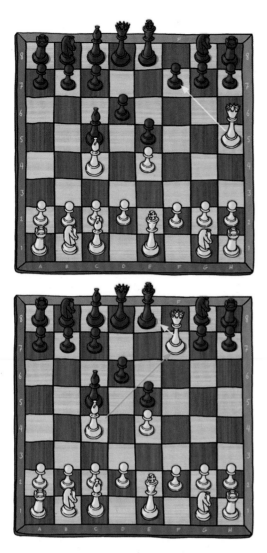

Now the queen can capture the black pawn standing one square diagonally in front of the black king.

The white queen is threatening the black king. The black king cannot capture the queen because she is protected by the white knight (see p. 19 for more information on the exchange). The king cannot move either because the white queen is threatening all the squares surrounding the king. The black king is in scholar's mate. Even though the game has only lasted for four moves, the game is over!

What went wrong for black? Let's rewind a few moves.

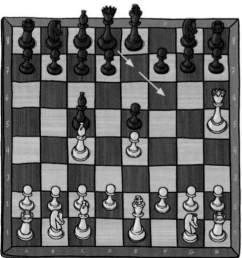

After white moved its queen, black should have responded by moving its queen one or two steps to cover the pawn. Moving the pawn one square in front of the queen was a blunder (see p. 19 for more information on blunders).

Indian Saying
"Chess is like an ocean where a mosquito can eat and an elephant can swim."

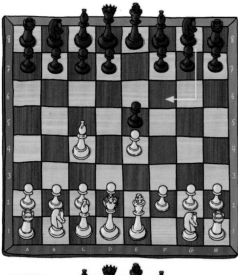

Rewind even a few more moves back.

After white moved its bishop, black should have moved its knight as shown.

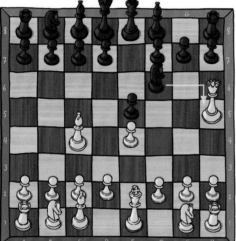

If the queen moves out now, the knight can capture her.

Now you have learned both how to place a scholar's mate and how to stop it. It's a lot of fun to win with just a few moves, but if you are playing against someone who knows how to stop the scholar's mate, your queen might get into trouble being out in the game this early. You will learn more about this in this in the Smart Opening Moves chapter (p. 113).

Oops!
Scholar's mate is a good weapon to have against beginners, but as you become a better player and meet stronger opponents, there is no use in even trying this move. Scholar's mate only works when your opponent is making mistakes.

Fool's Mate: The Quickest Mate

Fool's mate is the quickest mate. To accomplish fool's mate, your opponent has to be a terrible player with very little knowledge of the game.

White has played poorly and moved its pawns in a way that has left the area around the king wide open.

In just two moves, the black queen can move in a way that will threaten the king and he can even be put in checkmate! This is the quickest way to end a chess game.

> **Chess in Schools**
> In Armenia, it is obligatory for students in middle school to learn chess. All children from the age of six and up have chess classes two hours a week. The school system argues that chess contributes to "strengthen the children's intellectual minds" and helps their brains to be flexible and wise.

CHESS CHECK 21

Which pieces do you need to play the "stair mate"?

A) Two bishops

B) Two rooks

C) Two knights

CHESS CHECK 22

Which pieces are collaborating when playing scholar's mate?

A) A pawn and two rooks

B) The queen and the bishop that moves on the white squares

C) Two knights

CHESS CHECK 23

On what row can you put corridor mate?

A) The last row

B) The sixth row

C) The fifth row

(Answer Key p. 167)

Do You Remember the Mates?

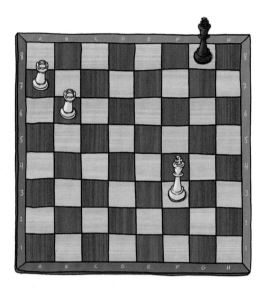

Now you have learned some of the most common mates. Do you remember them all? In the following scenarios, white is checkmating black. The answer key is on p. 167.

1. Place the two rooks mate.

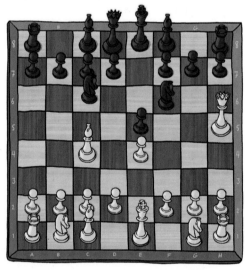

2. Place the scholar's mate.

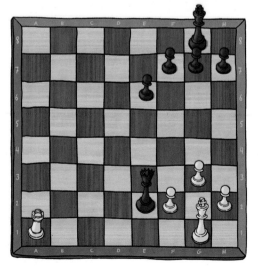

3. Place the corridor mate.

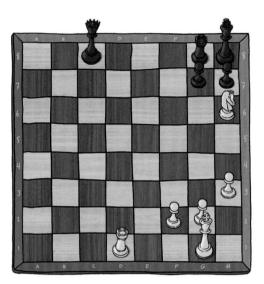

4. Place the smothered mate.

The Chess Dog

One of the members of the Brighton Chess Club in England in the 1930s was the nice Lady Sidney who always brought her dog Mick to the club. In fact, the rules actually prohibited animals in the building, but nobody had ever dared to tell Lady Sidney, until one day when the club got a new secretary.

Lady Sidney yelled at the new club secretary and the whole incident ended up in a compromise. Mick would be allowed in the building only if he became a member of the chess club. Later, Brighton was participating in a team match and the new team captain had discovered there was a new member on the list. He decided to add Mick on the club's third team. How do you think they did? Mick lost—his time ran out.

Can You Find the Mate?

To become the king of chess, it is smart to master the checkmate. Here you have eight exercises from some of the world champions' games.

When it says white's move or black's move, it means that it is white or black's turn to make a move. In each exercise, you can checkmate your opponent in one move. If you get stuck, you can look at the answer key on p. 168, but don't peek at the answers until you have tried to solve it by yourself!

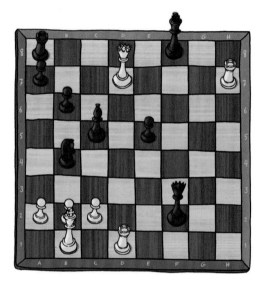

1. Mikhail Tal verus Josif Zilber (1949)

White's move.

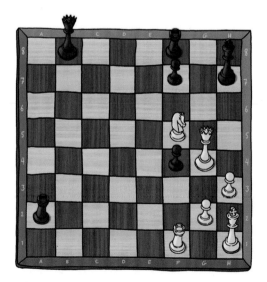

2. Viswanathan Anand versus Deen Hergott (1984)

White's move.

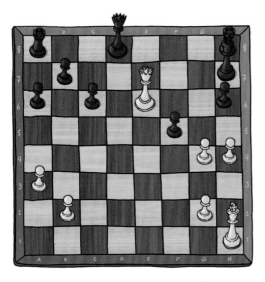

3. Wilhelm Steinitz versus NN (1861)

White's move.

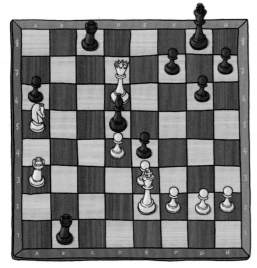

4. Victor Goglidze versus Mikhail Botvinnik (1935)

Black's move.

5. Emanuel Lasker versus Meyer (1900)

White's move.

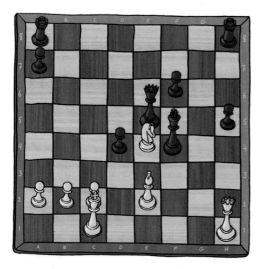

6. Anatolij Karpov versus Victor Kortsjnoj (1971)

White's move.

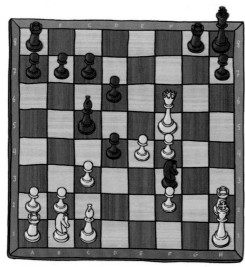

7. Reiner versus Wilhelm Steinitz (1860)

Black's move.

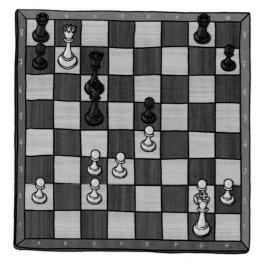

8. José Raúl Capablanca versus Herman Steiner (1933)

White's move.

Draws

Sometimes a game ends with a draw. There are several different things that can lead to a game ending with a draw:

- there are no pieces left that can checkmate
- stalemate (see p. 54)
- threefold repetition (see p. 55)
- fifty-move rule: when in the last fifty successive moves made by both players no pawns have moved and no captures have been made
- agree to a draw

Remis is the French word for tie.

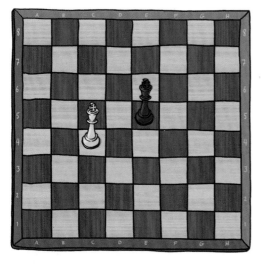

Here both white and black have only one piece left and those pieces are both kings. Neither one can checkmate the other, so the game is a draw.

Did you know that it is impossible to checkmate the king with one bishop or one knight left on the board? Nor is it possible to checkmate the king when the only pieces left are two knights (unless your opponent blunders!).

FIDE: World Chess Federation
Approximately 160 countries are members of the World Chess Federation–FIDE. Their motto is *Gens una sumus*, which means *We are one people*. The FIDE arranges tournaments like the World Chess Championship and the Chess Olympiad, calculates ratings, defines the rules of chess, and awards titles like grandmaster.

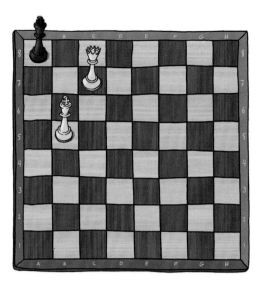

Stalemates occur when a player has no legal moves, but is not in check.

Black is in stalemate. The black king is not threatened, but has no squares he can legally move to.

Did you know that a game of chess can have three different outcomes? A win, a loss, or a draw. In chess tournaments you usually get one point for a win, half of a point for a draw, and no points for a loss.

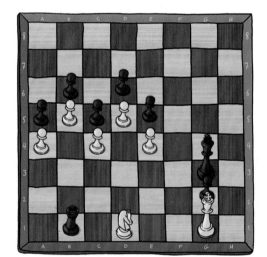

Stalemates can occur even when there are more pieces than just the king left on the board.

White has many pieces left, but is still in stalemate because he has no legal moves he can make. All the pawns are blocked, the king is not allowed to move anywhere, and the knight is stuck because if he moves, he is putting the white king into check.

No check—no checkmate!

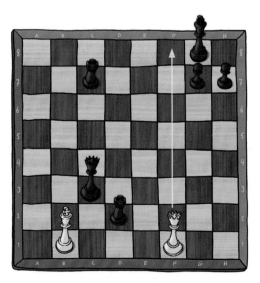

Sometimes stalemates can be a relief for a player who is in trouble. Here white is really stuck, but is the game over?

No! If the white queen was gone, the white king would become stalemate. White can move the queen to the square next to the black king. The black king has to capture the white queen.

54

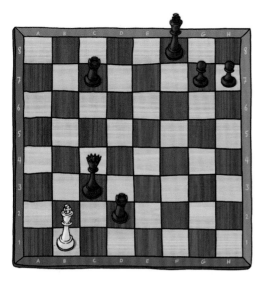

Now white is stalemate! Even if black is leading big time, stalemate occurred because white is not in check and cannot make any legal moves. This is good for white, not so good for black.

Chess player Dr. Savielly Tartakower once said: "No game has ever been won by giving up."

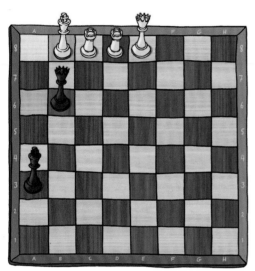

The threefold repetition rule applies when the same position occurs three times with the same player.

The black queen has put the white king in eternal chess by moving back and forth on the green squares. The white king has no other choice but to move back and forth on the yellow squares. The threefold repetition rule applies to this game.

Threefold repetition rule can also apply to a game if the players agree to it. Usually one of the players offers the other player a draw. The player who is offered the draw decides whether or not they wish to end the game immediately, or if they want to continue the game.

Naked Spectator
Right after World War II had ended, a huge chess tournament was interrupted by a spectator stripping naked. All the games were stopped, and the naked man was kicked out of the area. The tournament continued, but, shortly after, the man came back, and stripped naked once again. The games had to be stopped, and the man was sent back to his hotel room. A few minutes later, the game was interrupted once again by the same man stripping naked. This time he was standing in his hotel room window. Dr. Tartakower, one of history's funniest grandmasters, then demanded the threefold repetition rule to be applied to the games.

CHESS CHECK 24

What does *remis* mean?

A) White has won

B) Black has won

C) Draw

CHESS CHECK 25

What is a stalemate?

A) The king is threatened

B) A player has no legal moves to make and is not in check

C) A smart mate

CHESS CHECK 26

Who wins when there is a stalemate?

A) White

B) Nobody—the game ends with a draw

C) Whoever has the most remaining pieces

An Unusual Habit
Did you hear about the American named Oscar Tenner who had the bad habit of eating his chess pieces? Tenner was an inmate during World War I and did not have access to any chessboards while in prison. He got one meal a day, and he shaped the bread he was served into chess pieces.

Did you know that chess was the most popular board game among the warlords in Europe during the Middle Ages? In the 20th century, chess became a popular game played by millions of regular people as well. Today, chess is a game for everyone!

Did you know the most common reason for a remis is that both players agree to a draw?

(Answer Key p. 167)

En Passant: A Tricky, Special Rule

En passant is French and means *in passing*. If a pawn moves two steps forward at the start of the game, and it moves across a square that is threatened by one of the opponent's pawns, the opponent's pawn is allowed to move one square diagonally toward the just-moved pawn and capture it. En passant has to be done immediately after a pawn has passed a threatening square. This rule makes sure that pawns always will have a chance to capture other pawns as they pass them.

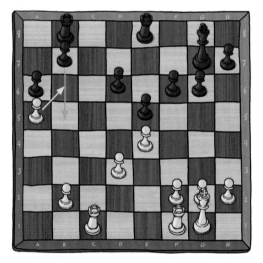

If black moves the pawn two steps forward, white can capture the pawn placed one square diagonally from white pawn. This is called en passant.

This is how it looks like after white has completed en passant.

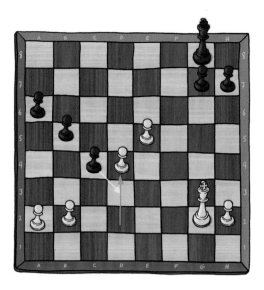

The white pawn just moved two steps and passed a square that was threatened by one of the black pawns. The black pawn can now capture the white pawn placed one square diagonally from it.

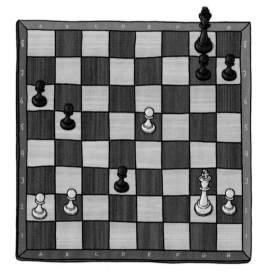

This is what it looks like after the black pawn has completed en passant.

Did you know that French chess terms such as *remis* and *en passant* originate from the 19th century? During that time, the majority of chess players were of the upper class. French was considered the "nice" language. Because of this, many countries that did not speak French adopted the nice French terms.

Chess Notation

Have you ever attempted to read the chess column in a newspaper, but given up because you couldn't understand the cryptic codes? Well, you are not alone. But don't worry—you are about to be introduced to the world of chess notation. You will be surprised by how easy it actually is.

Have you noticed the letters and numbers written on your chessboard? The lines contain the letters A–H, and the rows contain the numbers 1–8. Every square has its own identifying "name," which we can learn by looking at these letters and numbers. When we name a square, we read the letter first, then the number.

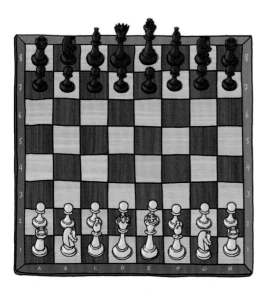

The green square is called e4. This is because it lies on the line labeled E, and the row labeled 4. When the moves in a game of chess are noted, both the black and white moves have to be noted. This way you will know exactly how many moves have been made, and you can play through the same moves later.

When a pawn moves, we only note the square it has moved to. If the white pawn starts at e2 and moves to e4, we only write e4.

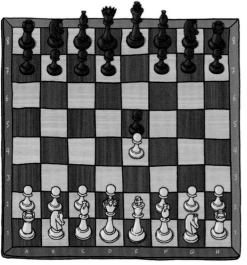

Many games start with both players moving their pawns two squares in front of the king.

White played e4, black played e5. In tournaments, a notation sheet is handed out containing the numbered moves. The moves have to be written on the same line. Like this: 1 e4 e5

In notation, both the players' moves are calculated together as one move.

When pieces other than pawns move, their first letter has to be added to the notation. We write:

B = bishop
N = knight
R = rook
Q = queen
K = king

If the white knight moves to c3 in the next move, this would be noted as Nc3. Simple, right?

Only one move has been made here. This move is called Nf3.

When a piece captures another piece, we write that as x. In chess notation this means captured.

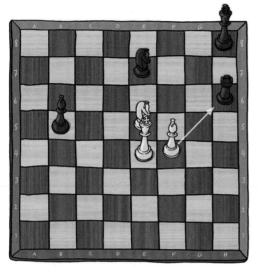

This move is called Bxh6.

If the opponent's king is placed in check, the move that was made is noted with a plus sign at the end. If it is a checkmate, the move is noted with a double plus ++.

Castling short is written 0-0. Castling long is written 0-0-0.

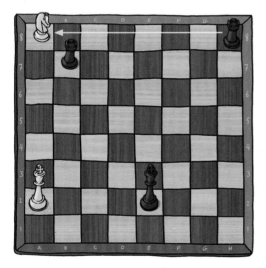

Black puts white in checkmate. This move is called Rxa8++.

If there are two equal pieces that can move to the same square, one has to note which one of the pieces made the move.

A Chessboard Accident
Grandmaster Aron Nimzowitsch once did a headstand during a tournament. What do you think happened? He fell down and broke his leg!

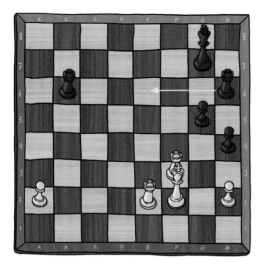

Black is moving its rook to e6. But black has another rook that can move to the same square, therefore the move has to be noted by the rook that made the move. Since the rook that made the move previously stood in the line H, this move is called Rhe6.

Tournaments are required to have notation. When a game is over, the result is noted on the notation sheet. If white won, the game is noted 0–1. If the game ended with a draw, it is noted as ½–½.

When you have learned chess notation, you can repeat games that were played over a century ago. In this way, a game of chess can live on forever. One of the most famous chess games was played in 1851 and is called "The Immortal Game." Practice chess notation, and you too can play the world-famous game!

White: Adolf Anderssen *Black:* Lionel Kieseritskij

1.	e4 e5
2.	f4 exf4
3.	Bc4 Qh4+
4.	Kf1 b5
5.	Bxb5 Nf6
6.	Nf3 Qh6
7.	d3 Nh5
8.	Nh4 Qg5
9.	Nf5 c6
10.	g4 Nf6
11.	Rg1 cxb5
12.	h4 Qg6
13.	h5 Qg5
14.	Df3 Ng8
15.	Bxf4 Qf6
16.	Nc3 Rc5
17.	Nd5 Qxb2
18.	Rd6 Rxg1
19.	e5 Qxa1
20.	Ke2 Na6
21.	Nxg7+ Kd8
22.	Qf6+ Nxf6
23.	Be7++

Game Analysis

After finishing a game where the moves have been noted, you may want to analyze the game. This is done by studying all the moves that you made, seeing which were good and which you could have done better. It is not uncommon for opponents to analyze their game together.

GRANDMASTER TIP

A good way to become a better chess player is to analyze your own games.

FRANCISCO VALLEJO PONS, SPAIN

If you still find chess notation complicated, it might be a comfort to know that chess notation was much harder back in the day. In *Lucenas*, a chess book from the 15th century, we find the move: *Jugar del peon del rey a IIII casa, que se entiende contando de donde esta el rey.*

Today this move is called e4.

Did you know that there are several different symbols we can put after the moves when analyzing a game, depending on whether we find the move good or bad?

! Means a good move
!! Means a very good move
? Means a bad move
?? Means a very bad move

Petrosjan's blunder on p. 20 got a ?? after the move.

CHESS CHECK 27

Many tournaments are required to...?

A) ... call out the moves

B) ... note the moves

C) ... hide the moves

CHESS CHECK 28

What are the four squares in the middle of the board called?

A) a1, b1, c1, d1

B) e4, d4, e5, d5

C) h5, h6, h7, h8

CHESS CHECK 29

What rows do the pawns always start at?

A) Row 2 for white and row 7 for black

B) Row 1 for white and row 2 for black

C) Row 1 for white and row 8 for black

(Answer Key p. 167)

Hunting Pieces

Having more and better pieces than your opponent is always a good thing. You should therefore look for opportunities where you can hunt your opponent's pieces. It's easier to lead an army that is bigger than the enemy's. It's easier to checkmate someone when you have more pieces on the offensive than the opponent has on the defensive.

Did you know that you are only allowed to use one hand at a time when you play chess? You have to press the watch with the same hand that you made a move with.

Did you know that chess is often called "the royal game"?

Destroy Their Defense

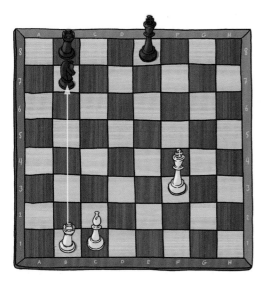

The white rook is threatening the black knight. White does not want to capture the knight because the rook will then be captured in the next move. If you manage to threaten away the black rook, knight will be left alone with no cover. Can you figure out how to do this?

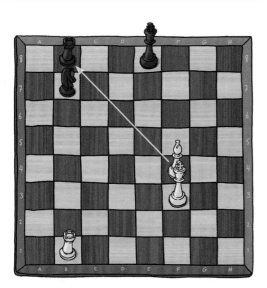

The bishop moves to f4 and is threatening the black rook. The rook should now move, and you can capture the black knight with your rook in your next move.

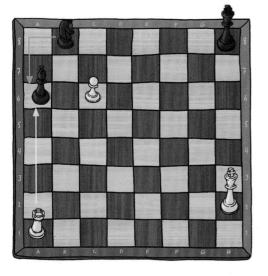

The white rook is threatening the black bishop. The only piece that is covering for the bishop is the black knight. Can you destroy the bishop's defense?

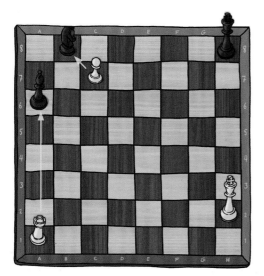

If you move the pawn to c7, you will be threatening the black knight. Black will need to move the knight so it avoids getting captured, but in doing so the bishop's defense will also disappear. No matter what black decides to do, white will capture one of its pieces.

Loose Officers

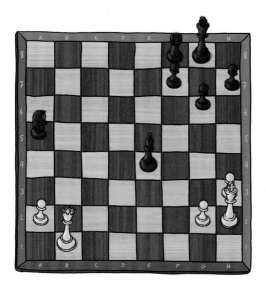

The queen, rooks, bishops, and knights are all called officers. A loose officer is an officer that is not covered, and that is placed in a threatening situation.

Black has two loose officers: the knight and the bishop. Can you find a way for white to threaten both of the pieces at once?

On e1, the queen is threatening both the officers. Black can only save one of them, and white wins one piece.

66

An Annoying Opponent

During a game in 1977, Tigran Petrosjan shook the chessboard while he was playing against Viktor Kortsjnoj. Kortsjnoj got annoyed and asked Petrosjan to stop. Petrosjan then turned off his hearing aid. Kortsjnoj became furious and responded by kicking Petrosjan under the table. To avoid further kicks, the tournament board decided to put up a partition wall underneath the table for the next game.

Catching Pieces

One of the black officers is not threatened, but there are no squares that it can move to without being threatened by one of the white pawns. Can you identify the black officer?

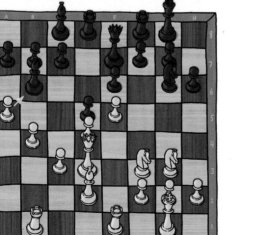

It is the black bishop on b6. White is taking advantage of the situation and moves the pawn to a5, where it is now threatening the bishop. The bishop is trapped! No matter what it does, it will be captured by one of the white pawns.

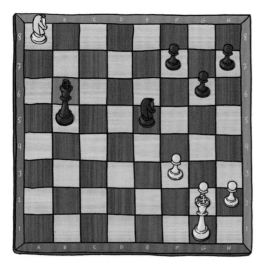

The white knight has two options: b6 and c7. But c7 is the only safe move, as b6 is threatened by the black king.

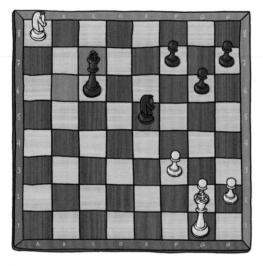

Black moves its king to c6. Now the knight is not safe on c7 either. The knight is in trouble! White has to move one of the other pieces.

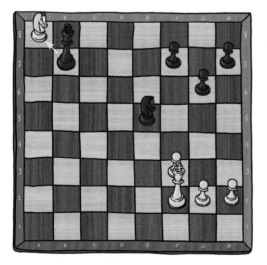

Black king moves to b7 and is threatening the knight. The white knight is trapped. No matter where it moves, it will be captured by the black king.

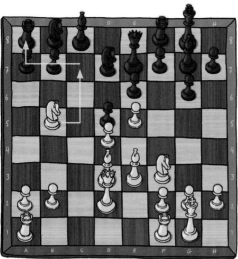

If the rook remains in his corner position, he might get captured.

White can move the knight to c7. It will then be threatening the black rook. The rook is trapped, and the white knight can capture it in its next move.

A Chess-Playing Machine

In 1769, inventor Wolfgang von Kempelen proudly presented his chess-playing machine, known as "The Turk." The machine was human-sized, dressed as a Turk, and strapped to a rolling cabinet with a chessboard placed on top. One of the Turk's greatest challengers was Napoleon himself. A lot of people found themselves astonished by the mechanical miracle. But it was all a big bluff, because inside of the machine there was a man making all of the Turk's moves. One of the men who controlled the Turk was Johann Allgaier, one of the best chess players at the time. The Turk went on tours in Cuba and the United States. Eventually it ended up in a museum in Philadelphia, where it was destroyed in a fire in 1854.

Watch Out for Overloaded Pieces

Overloading is when a piece has too many duties at once. A duty is often to protect another piece.

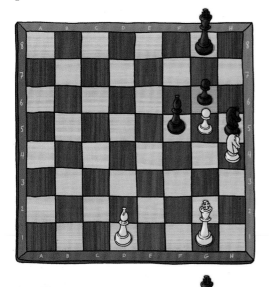

The black pawn is overloaded.

The pawn is the only piece that is protecting the black bishop and the black knight. White is threatening both of these pieces and can capture one of them. The only way the black pawn can get back at white is by giving up the protection of one of the other pieces.

If the white bishop captures the knight on h5, and black responds by capturing the white pawn, white can capture the black bishop with its knight in the next move.

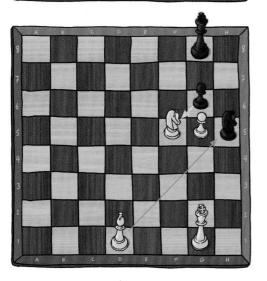

If white decides to capture the bishop on f5 with its knight instead, and black responds with capturing the pawn, white can capture the knight on h5 with its bishop. White wins one piece because the pawn on g6 is overloaded.

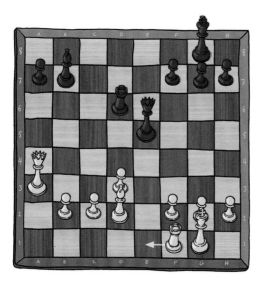

The only piece protecting the black rook is the queen.

The rook moves to e1 and threatens the queen.

Did you know that some people in France once used to say "Madame" when they were threatening the opponent's queen?

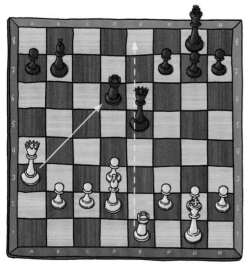

The black queen is now overloaded.

It has to cover for both the rook and square e8 to prevent the white rook from placing the king in corridor mate (see p. 41). The queen is unable to do both jobs, and black is therefore losing a piece.

Brutal Indians
Around the year 950 there was a group of Indian chess players who used to play with an unusual bet. The loser had to chop off a body part! They would start with a finger. When all the fingers were chopped off, they continued with arms and legs. After some time it must have been very difficult to move the chess pieces.

Correspondence Chess

Correspondence chess is chess played over a long distance. This has traditionally been done over letters, where each move is sent as a letter or a postcard. It has become more common to transmit the moves by e-mail or in other ways over the Internet.

Correspondence chess games often take a long time to finish. Even though the games are played with limited thinking time, it can take several years to finish a game. It has even happened that one of the players has died before finishing the game!

Tactical Tips

The two most important skills in chess are tactics and strategy. Tactics in chess refers to a chosen move sequence that will help you in the game. The end goal can be the capture of a piece, putting your opponent's king in checkmate, or reaching a draw when you cannot win. The outcomes of many chess games are determined by tactical tricks. Here are some tactical weapons.

Fork

When a piece is threatening two of its opponent's pieces simultaneously, it is called a fork. This is a smart double attack that can win you a piece, as the opponent can only save one of the threatened pieces. All pieces can fork.

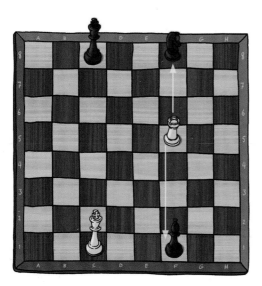

The white rook has forked the black bishop and knight.

It is particularly smart to fork the opponent's king and another piece. Because the king is threatened, it has to be saved, and you can then capture the other piece that is threatened.

According to chess expert Teichman, chess is 99 percent tactics!

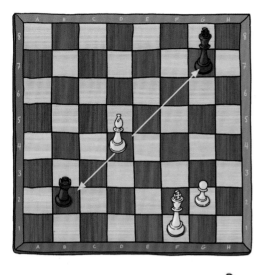

The white bishop has forked the black king and rook.

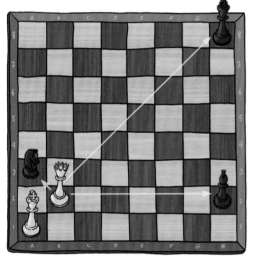

The white queen has forked the black king, bishop, and knight.

The knight is particularly good at forking. If a piece is threatening three or more pieces simultaneously, it is called a family fork.

Grandmaster Dr. Savielly Tartakower summed up tactics as follows: "The tactic needs to know what needs to be done when there is something that needs to be done, and the strategist needs to know what needs to be done when there is nothing that needs to be done."

Do you get it?

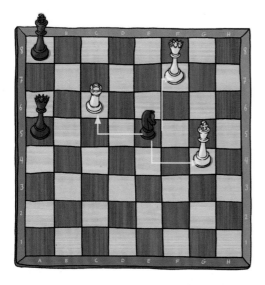

The black knight has family forked the white king, queen, and rook.

Pawns can fork as well.

The white pawn on c6 is forking the black rook and knight.

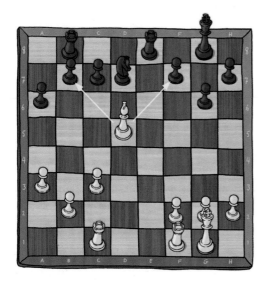

The white bishop is threatening two pieces, the pawn on b7 and the pawn on f7.

However, this is not a fork! Both pawns are covered, and it would not be smart of the bishop to capture them. In order for it to be a fork, you have to gain something by forking.

Pins

A piece is pinned if it is trapped on a square where it either cannot or should not move because there is a more valuable piece standing behind it. When a piece is pinned because the king is behind it, it is an absolute pin. The piece is then not allowed to move. When a piece is pinned because a piece other than the king is placed behind it, it is allowed to move, but it is often a bad decision.

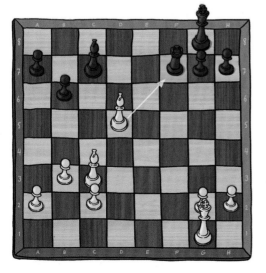

The black rook is pinned by the white bishop. The rook is absolute pinned, and is not allowed to move because that would put the black king under threat.

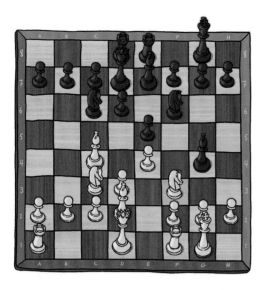

The white knight is pinned by the black bishop. The knight is allowed to move, but it would not be a very smart move. Do you see why? Because the black bishop can capture the white queen.

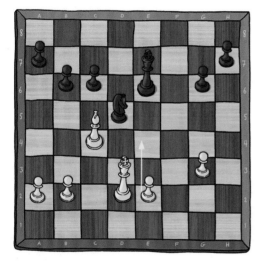

If you have pinned one of your opponent's pieces, it is smart to try and threaten it with another piece.

The white bishop has pinned the black knight. White can move its pawn to e4. There he is threatening the knight, and you can capture the knight with your pawn in your next move.

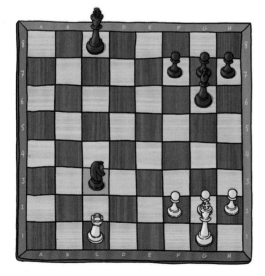

The black knight is in an absolute pin. It is not allowed to move because it will then put its own king in check.

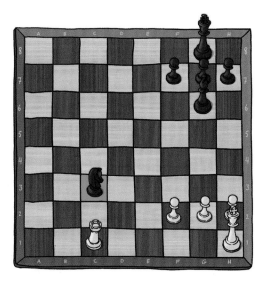

There are no pieces placed behind the knight, but it is pinned anyways. Do you see why?

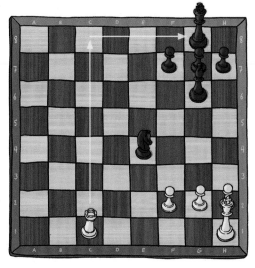

If the knight moves, the white rook can move to c8 and put the king in corridor mate!

Simple tips about pins:
- always be on the lookout for different ways you can pin your opponent's pieces
- if you have pinned a piece, it is smart to get more pieces to threaten the pinned piece
- try to avoid letting your pieces get pinned

A Chess Champion on the National Soccer Team

Grandmaster Simen Agdestein is a champion of multiple talents. In addition to being an amazing chess player, he is also on the national soccer team. There are not too many people who can brag about playing on two national sports teams at the same time!

GRANDMASTER TIP
To become a good chess player, it is smart to stay physically active.
MAGNUS CARLSEN, NORWAY
WORLD CHAMPION, 2013

Discovered Attack

A discovered attack gives you the opportunity to capture your opponent's pieces. A discovered attack takes place if you move a piece out of the way of another and the revealed piece can attack.

The white bishop moves to h7. The black king is now in check. In addition, it is revealed that the white queen can attack the black queen. Black has to do something with the check, and white can capture the queen in its next move.

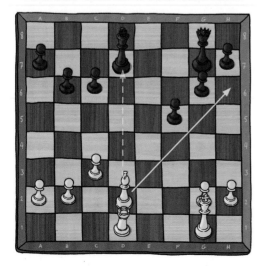

White moves the bishop to h6. The bishop is now threatening the black queen, and simultaneously the white rook is threatening the king. This is called a discovered check.

When you put a king in a discovered check, it's almost like you are doing two moves at once.

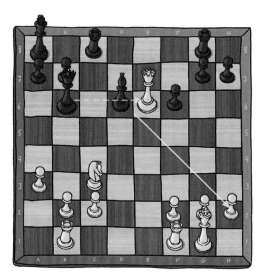

Black is moving its bishop and captures the pawn on h2. The bishop has now put the white king in check. When the bishop moves, it clears the way for an attack along the sixth row. The black queen is threatening the white queen. White needs to do something with the check, and black can capture the white queen in its next move.

Windmill

With the help of a discovered attack, you can do a smart trick called the windmill.

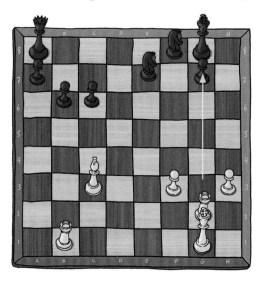

Black is in the lead by a few pieces, but, with the help of the windmill, white can win almost all the black pieces, one by one. The white rook captures the pawn on g7 and threatens the black king. The white bishop covers the rook, so that the black king is unable to capture it. The king needs to move and has only one square to go to, h8.

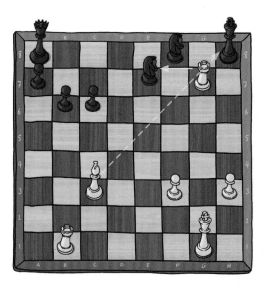

The white rook captures the knight on e7. This clears the way for the bishop on c3, which is threatening the black king. The king needs to move back to g8.

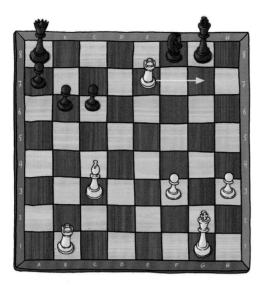

White moves the rook back to g7 and threatens the black king. The black king needs to move back to h8 again. Can you tell what is going to happen next with white?

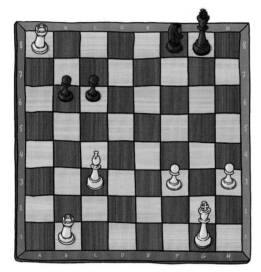

The white rook captures the black bishop and clears the way again for the white bishop, which is now threatening the black king. The black king needs to move to g8 once again.

White takes advantage of the discovered attack that takes place every time the black king is back on h8, and uses the rook to eat up all of the black pieces placed on the seventh row, one by one. Eventually it will capture the black queen.

White has almost captured all the black pieces with the help of the windmill.

Double Check

Double check is when two pieces simultaneously are threatening the opponent's king. The only way you can achieve double check is with the help of a discovered attack. When you double check, it is of no help for your opponent to capture one of the checking pieces. The king will still be in check. Double check can therefore be very dangerous, as the only piece that is allowed to move is the king.

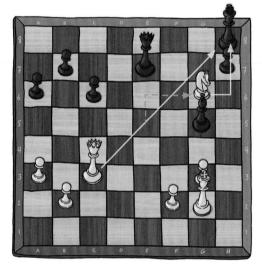

White just moved its knight from e5 to g6. The white knight and queen have double checked the black king.

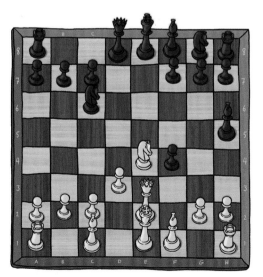

With the help of a double check, you sometimes accomplish a checkmate.

    The white queen can capture the black bishop on h5. But white can also do a lot better—do you see how?

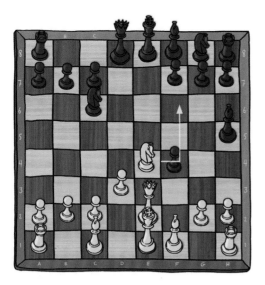

White can move its knight to f6 and double check the king with the queen and knight.

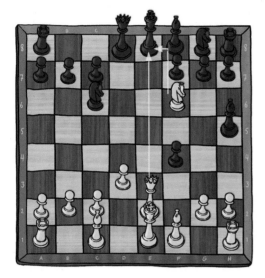

That is even a checkmate!

Simple tips about discovered attacks:
- they create opportunities for you to win one or more of your opponent's pieces
- they are extra scary when they are threatening the opponent's king
- sometimes they can lead to a checkmate

Generous Chess Champions
When Kasparov played Karpov during the 1986 World Championship, they were playing for over $700,000. The two champions generously donated all their winnings to charity in the Ukraine as the big Chernobyl disaster had happened the same year.

Skewer

A skewer is an attack of two pieces placed on the same line or on the same diagonal. The most valuable piece is placed in front of a piece with similar or less value. Your opponent is forced to move the most valuable piece to avoid it getting captured. You can then capture the less valuable piece. The pieces that can skewer are the queen, rooks, and bishops.

The white bishop is threatening the black king. When the king moves, the bishop can capture the black queen. The bishop skewered the king and the queen.

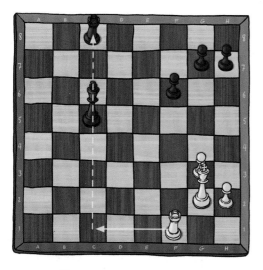

The rook is also good at skewering.

White moves the rook to c1. It is now skewering the black king and rook. The white rook is threatening the black rook through the black king. The king needs to move away from the C line, and in the next move white can capture the black rook. You can skewer an opponent when they have pieces placed on the same line, row, or diagonal.

Here there are only a few pieces left on the board. Black has two important pieces placed on the same line. Do you see what white can do?

The white queen can move to b1, where it will be placed on the same line as the black pieces. The black king has to get out of the B line, and white can then in the next move capture the black queen.

Murder on the Chessboard
Today chess is a peaceful game, but it has not always been so. In 1254, William of Wendene stabbed his opponent to death during a game of chess.

86

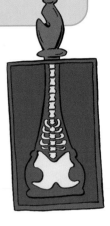

X-ray Attack

Have you ever taken an x-ray? In chess, we have something called an x-ray attack. This is when you are threatening a piece through one of your other pieces.

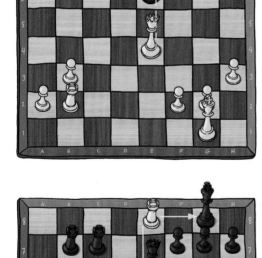

The white rook on a8 is threatening the black knight. The black queen is covering the knight. The white queen is threatening the black knight through the black queen.

The white rook can capture the knight and fork the black king and queen.

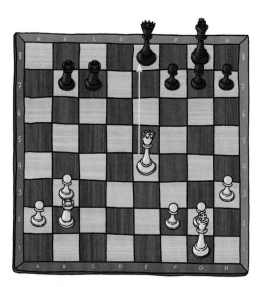

Black has only one legal move to make: to capture the rook. In the next move, white queen will capture the black queen and put the king in corridor mate.

GRANDMASTER TIP

The pieces are your friends! So be considerate of them while you are playing. The queen is a demanding lady; although she is good at multitasking, she needs some room to do so. The king needs protection. Do not let him out to fight until the streets are safe (during the end game). The rook is made for offense, not defense. The bishop is like a colorblind sniper who is very good when working together with your other sniper. The knight is scary and erratic, like a spy. It is at its best when kept on a fixed point. The pawns are the game's troopers and can never move backward. You should therefore think carefully before deciding to move them.

SUNE BERG HANSEN, DENMARK

The Sacrifice: Give Some, Gain More

To sacrifice a piece means that a player lets their opponent capture a piece knowing that the move will help them to make an attack move next. Here are three good victims.

Deflection Sacrifice

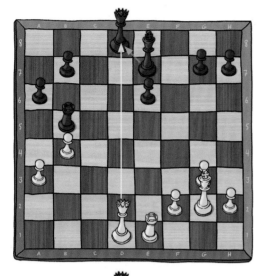

When we make a sacrifice, we force an opponent's piece to move away from a particular square.

It is white's turn. The white queen is threatening the black queen. The black king is the only piece covering the queen. If you can force the king away from his square, you can capture the queen. Do you see how white can divert the black king?

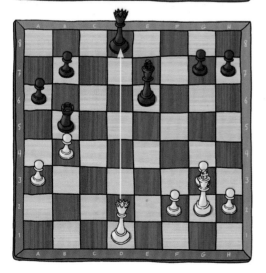

The white rook captures the pawn on e6. The king is now in check and has to move away from the queen, and the queen will be left unprotected.

The best thing the black king can do is to capture the white rook. The black queen is lost whatever black decides to do next.

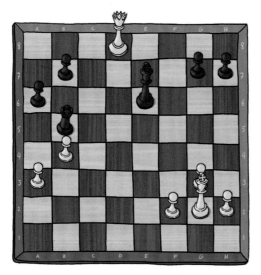

The white queen captures the black queen. White sacrificed Rxe6 to win the black queen. Let us take count of the pieces that got captured: White captured a pawn and the queen. Black captured a rook. That is a good trade for white!

Auspicious Cats

Former World Champion Alekhin was really fond of cats. He would often bring along one of his cats, or a photo or a cat figure, to his tournaments. He thought that if a cat walked on his chessboard before he started playing, it would bring him luck.

Magnet Sacrifice

In a magnet sacrifice you "pull" one of your opponent's pieces to a particular square. Magnet sacrifices can be used to make strong forks or pins.

The white rook moves to c8 and is threatening the black queen. Since the king is placed behind, the black queen is pinned to the eighth row. Black is out of options and is forced to capture the rook.

Do you see what white can do now?

White can move the knight to e7 and fork the black king and queen.

White did a magnet sacrifice that made it possible to set up the fork and capture the black queen.

Some magnet sacrifices can be good enough to win the game immediately.

The white rook moves to h8.

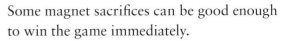

The black king is now threatened by the rook.

It looks like white has made a mistake and blundered its rook, but white has a plan!

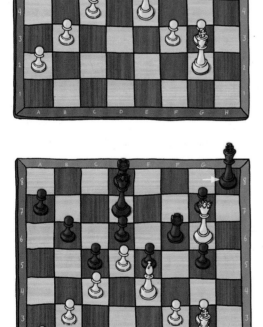

The black king captures the rook. Do you see what white can do now?

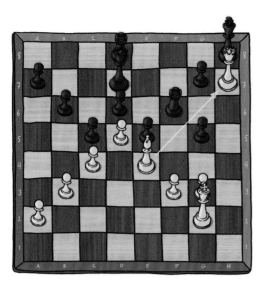

White can move the queen to h7 and checkmate the black king! It is impossible for the king to capture the queen as she is covered by the bishop. White sacrificed its rook to lure the king to h8 and then checkmate him.

Clearance Sacrifice

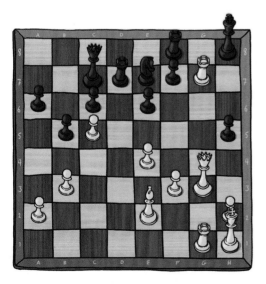

You might experience one of your own pieces blocking the way for a checkmate, or some other tactical move you wish to make. It is then often smart to clear the way by making a clearance sacrifice.

The black king is threatened. The area around him is open, and the white pieces have built up a strong attack. The white rook on g7 is blocking the way for the white queen. If it wasn't for the rook, the queen could have moved to g7 and checkmated the king. This is the perfect time for a clearance sacrifice!

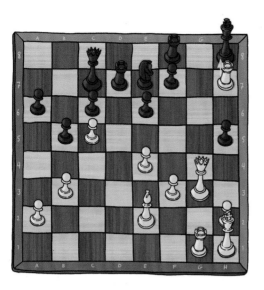

The rook is clearing the way by moving to h7. The black king is now put in check, and the only legal move he has is to capture the white rook.

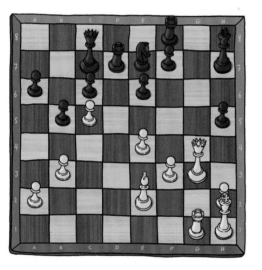

Do you see what white can do now?

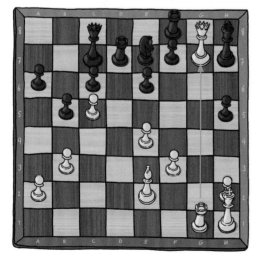

The area around the queen is no longer blocked and she can move to g7. The black king is unable to move as the queen is now threatening every possible move he can make. And black cannot capture the queen as she is covered by the rook. That is checkmate!

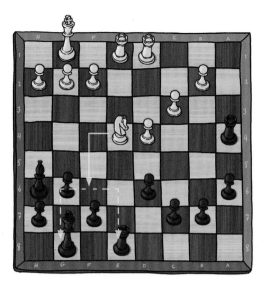

To be able to fend off an opponent's tactical possibilities is just as important as taking advantage of your own tactical possibilities.

It is black's turn. The white knight is threatening by the possibility of moving to f6 and forking the black king and rook on e8. How can black fend off this threat?

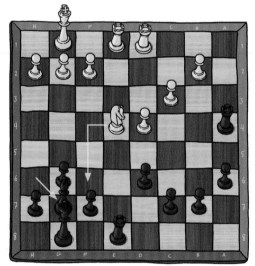

Black can stop the fork from happening by moving its bishop to g7 so that it will be covering f6, or by moving its rook or king. Even though black has several opportunities to avoid the fork, he or she needs to watch out so that no other tactical traps will take place.

If black moves the bishop to g7, white moves the knight to f6.

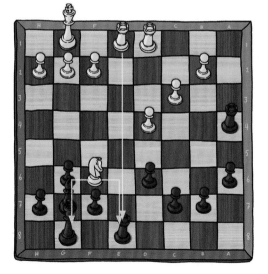

White has a double threat. The knight is threatening the king, and the white rook is threatening the black rook.

No matter what black does, white will win a piece.

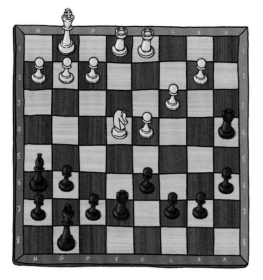

If black moves the rook to e7, a new tactical possibility is created for white.

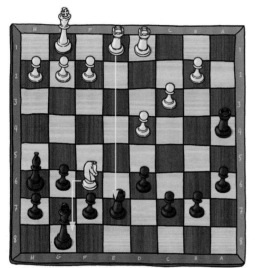

The knight can make a deflection sacrifice on f6.

Both the king and the rook are threatened. Black has to move the king to f8 to protect the rook.

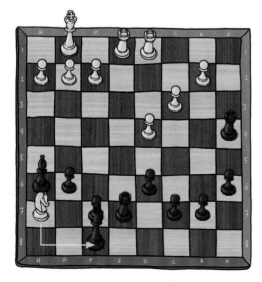

White captures the pawn on h7 and simultaneously creates a check. In order for the king to continue protect the rook, he needs to move to e8.

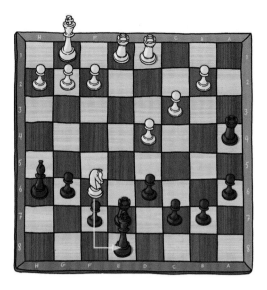

White moves the knight back to f6 and is threatening the black king.

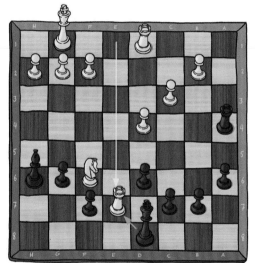

No matter where the black king moves, white will win a piece.

White captures the rook, and black retaliates with the king.

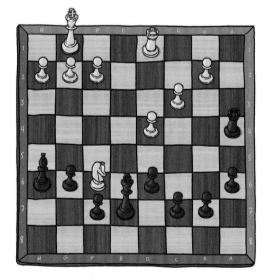

Do you see what white can do now?

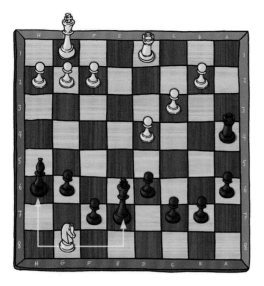

The knight can move to g8 and fork the king and the bishop.

Imagine how annoying it is to have managed to avoid one fork, and then—with only one wrong move—the opponent has been given the opportunity for a discovered attack which then leads to another fork.

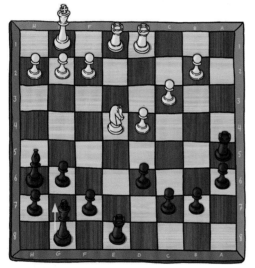

Let us rewind.

The best move black could have done to avoid the fork was to move the king to g7.

Although all chess games are different, you can use these tactical patterns in many of your games.

CHESS CHECK 30	CHESS CHECK 31	CHESS CHECK 32
What is it called when one piece is threatening two pieces at once? A) A skewer B) A discovered attack C) A fork	What is a pinned piece? A) A piece that cannot or should not move B) A captured piece C) A piece that is threatening the opponent's king	What does it mean to sacrifice a piece? A) To move it backward B) To exchange it with a piece of the same value C) To give away a piece to gain something better

(Answer Key p. 167)

Are You a Tactical Master?

A person who is a king at chess is good at solving tactical problems. Can you find the moves that the world champions found? In each scenario, your goal is to win a piece. You will have to look for opportunities for forks, skewers, discovered attacks, diversions, and pins. The answer key is on p. 169.

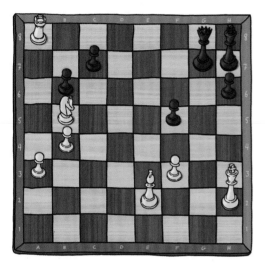

1. Mark Tajmanov versus Bobby Fischer (1971)

Black's move.

Can you find Fischer's family fork?

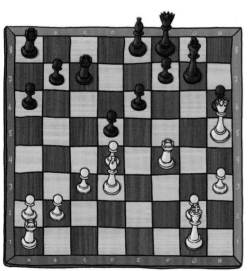

2. Mikhail Tal versus A. Leonov (1949)

White's move.

Win a rook with the help of a fork.

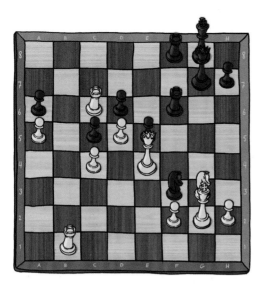

3. Bent Larsen versus Bobby Fischer (1971)

Black's move.

How did Fischer fork two valuable pieces?

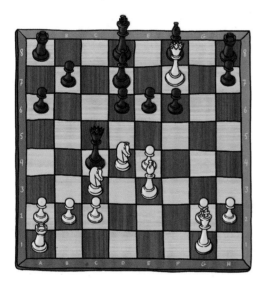

4. Emanuel Lasker versus Vesja Pirc (1935)

White's move.

Lasker won a rook with a fork. How?

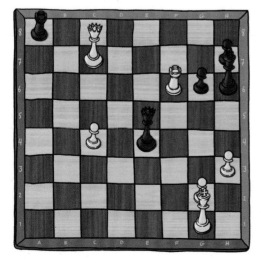

5. Mark Tajmanov versus Bobby Fischer (1971)

Black's move.

Win the rook with the help of a fork.

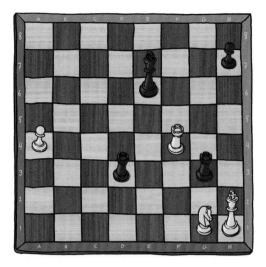

6. Boris Savtsjenko versus Vladimir Kramnik (2010)

Black's move.

Make a pin that will win a piece.

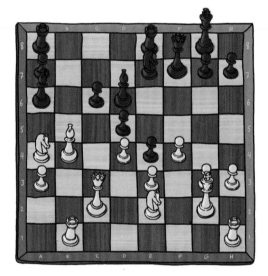

7. Dmitrij Gurevitsj versus Mikhail Tal (1988)

Black's move.

How did Tal pin two good pieces?

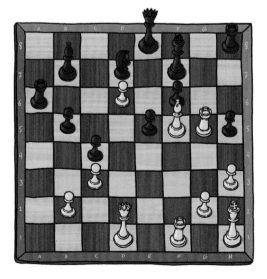

8. Mikhail Tal versus Boris Spasskij (1980)

White's move.

Skewer black's best and most important pieces.

9. van Hartingsvelt versus Max Euwe (1919)

Black's move.

Win white's queen with the help of a pin.

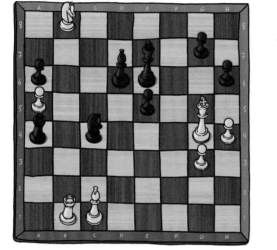

10. Max Bouaraba versus Rustam Kasimdz-hanov (2010)

Black's move.

Can you win a rook with the help of a discovered attack?

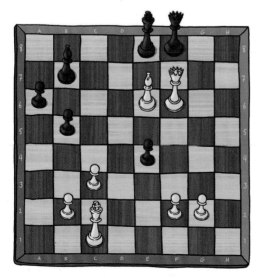

11. Garri Kasparov versus Vladimir Kramnikn (1994)

White's move.

Win black's queen with the help of a diversion victim.

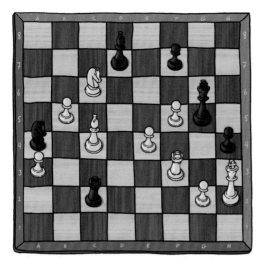

12. Magnus Carlsen versus Maxime Vachier-Lagrave (2010)

White's move.

How did Magnus fork two officers?

GRANDMASTER TIP
A good way to become better at chess is by solving several tactical problems.

JAN SMEETS, THE NETHERLANDS

Blindfold Chess

Blindfold chess is a form of chess play where the players are unable to see either the chessboard or the pieces during the game. The moves are communicated with the help of chess notation.

Blindfold chess is often played when there is a level difference between the players. The world's best chess players can play blindfold chess against multiple players at once. Norwegian Magnus Carlsen can play blindfold chess against thirty players simultaneously. Even with a blindfold covering his eyes, he is able to remember where all the pieces are placed in all of the games.

The Chess Player Aladdin

Did you think that Aladdin was only an adventurer and cartoon? No! At the end of the 14th century, Aladdin was considered the world's best chess players. His nickname was "Ali the Chess Player."

Aladdin impressed others by playing blindfold chess. And he happily played several games at once when he was playing regular chess.

World Champions and World Championship Games

In the 19th century, chess as a competitive game was expanding. The first modern chess tournament was arranged in 1851, and in 1886 we had our very first official world champion. The world championship in chess was originally arranged between the current world champion and a challenger. Since then, the championship has evolved into tournaments with several players. And now the championship is a cup tournament, better known as FIDE World Chess Championship.

To be a world champion in chess, the grand chess king, is a nice title. Today a lot of money is spent on arranging world championship matches. The games are shared online, so that they can be watched all over the world.

Uncontested World Champions

1. Wilhelm Steinitz, Austria, World Champion 1886–1894
Steinitz was the very first official World Champion in 1886. He defended the title three times over the next eight years.

Steinitz was once asked about his chances in a tournament he was going to play in. He answered, "Good," on the grounds that the other players had to play against Steinitz, something he did not have to do.

2. Emanuel Lasker, Germany, World Champion 1894–1921
Emanuel Lasker became World Champion in 1894. In addition to being a very strong player, he wrote philosophical texts and had a doctorate in mathematics.

Lasker was a good friend of the one and only Albert Einstein. Einstein wrote the preface for a biography of Lasker, where he described Lasker as one of the most interesting people he had met.

3. José Raúl Capablanca, Cuba, World Champion 1921–1927

Capablanca learned chess at the age of only four. He would watch his father play, and he won the very first game he played against him. Many people consider Capablanca the most gifted chess player of all time.

The Slimmest Chess Book
A book has been published containing all of the games that Capablanca ever lost. It is perhaps the world's slimmest chess book. In his eight-year-long career, he didn't lose a single game!

4. Aleksander Alekhin, Russia/France, World Champion 1927–1935, 1937–1946

At the age of seven, Alekhin was already almost possessed by chess. He would find his chessboard in the middle of the night and start playing. Alekhin became World Champion in 1927. He lost his title in 1935, but easily won it back two years later. He remained World Champion until 1946 and was preparing for a new World Championship match when he suddenly died in his hotel room in 1946 at only fifty-four years old.

During a tournament in Karlsbad in 1925, Alekhin spent his day off in a sensible way: he played blitz chess against Emanuel Lasker for 12 hours!

5. Max Euwe, the Netherlands, World Champion 1935–1937

Max Euwe was the man who beat Aleksander Alekhin in 1935. Euwe was Dutch and a huge star in his home country. He has written several textbooks about chess and was the president of FIDE.

6. Mikhail Botvinnik, USSR, World Champion 1948–1957, 1958–1960, 1961–1963

When Aleksander Alekhin died as current World Champion in 1946, a tournament was held with the five best players to elect a new World Champion. Mikhail Botvinnik won this tournament in 1948, and was then the sixth World Champion. He lost and won the title again twice. In addition to being a World Champion, Botvinnik took part in establishing a Russian chess school, which has trained some of the world's best chess players.

7. Vasilij Smyslov, USSR, World Champion 1957–1958

Smyslov became World Champion in 1957 when he beat Botvinnik. Smyslov looked at chess as an art form, not unlike music. In addition to playing chess, he was a gifted opera singer, but decided to focus on his chess career after an unsuccessful audition at the Bolsjoj Theatre. In addition to the World Champion title, he also won ten gold medals in the European Championship for teams and seventeen medals in the Chess Olympiad.

8. Mikhail Tal, USSR, World Champion 1960–1961

Mikhail Tal was nicknamed "The Wizard from Riga." Tal continuously surprised his opponents with dangerous attacks, smart traps, and brilliant sacrifices. Tal was a heavy smoker and struggled with bad health. Several times he had to cancel a tournament because of his health.

9. Tigran Petrosjan, USSR, World Champion 1963–1969

Petrosjan became World Champion in 1963 and kept the title until 1969. Petrosjan was a brilliant strategist. He was very good at taking advantage of his opponent's tiny mistakes. Petrosjan's game style led him to lose very few games, but many of his games ended in a draw.

10. Boris Spasskij, USSR, World Champion 1969–1972

Spasskij was known as a charming gentleman. He became a World Champion in 1969, and with this title he became the first double World Champion as he also held a Junior World Champion title from 1955. Spasskij was very athletic and would often play a game of tennis between the chess matches. Spasskij is most famous for the World Championship match against Bobby Fischer in 1972—which he lost.

11. Bobby Fischer, USA, World Champion 1972–1975

Robert James Fischer, better known as Bobby Fischer, is considered to be one of the most talented chess players of all time. As a teen, he was a world sensation. He gained a lot of attention when he became a Grandmaster at the age of fifteen.

Fischer became a World Champion in 1972 in Reykjavik, the capital of Iceland. But this title did not come easy. It was first after long negotiations concerning the place of championship and the prize money. The World Championship match created a lot of buzz in the media all over the world. Never before had chess gotten this much attention. The tournament was supposed to start July 2nd, but they were not even sure Fischer would show. The opening ceremony was held without him. He was still in his home in New York. The American association managed to delay the start of the first round of the tournament with the excuse that Fischer was feeling ill, and his story became the focus of the media. Was he going to show or not? Chess enthusiast and millionaire Jim Slater offered to double the prize money. Fischer agreed to play. When Fischer arrived in Reykjavik, he kept mostly to himself and sent one of his assistants as his representative during the lottery. The winning numbers would play white in the first round, and, according to the regulations, the players themselves had to be present. The match was once again delayed. Spasskij and the Soviet delegation were furious and demanded that Fischer forfeit his first game because of his absence. The disagreement was finally solved two days later after Fischer offered Spasskij a handwritten apology. The match was still delayed a few extra days though, because Fischer had to have a special chair flown from the United States, and he spent a lot of extra time accepting the chessboard and its pieces. But on July 11th, the Championship finally began.

After several days of games and additional scandal, Fischer eventually won the match. This took place during the Cold War. While Fischer arrived back in the United States as a hero, Spasskij received a much less warm welcome when he returned to the Soviet Union after his loss against the American. Fischer lost his World Champion title in 1975, when he refused to show up and defend his title.

12. Anatolij Karpov, USSR, World Champion 1975–1981

Karpov was announced as World Champion in 1975 after Fischer's refusal to show. Karpov had learned chess rules as a four year old. Each time he lost a game, he started crying. His dad would then firmly tell him that if he kept crying, they had to stop playing. At age seven, Karpov visited a chess club for the first time and excelled.

At age fifteen, a misunderstanding sent him to an international tournament. The Soviet Union had received an invitation to send two players. They thought it was a junior tournament and gave Karpov one of the spots. When he arrived, it turned out to be a senior tournament with several strong masters. Karpov surprised everyone by winning the entire tournament.

Karpov was also an avid stamp collector, and had a collection worth over 11 million dollars. He was also interested in politics, and was a member of the Russian National Assembly. In 2010, he stood for election as president of FIDE. He was supported by Magnus Carlsen and Garri Kasparov, among others, but lost the election. Karpov reigned over the world of chess for ten years.

13. Garri Kasparov, USSR/Russia, World Champion 1985–2000

Kasparov became the youngest World Champion of all time in 1985, when he beat Karpov in the World Championship. He remained World Champion from 1985 to 2000 and is considered one of the strongest chess players of all time. He held the rating record until Magnus Carlsen beat it in 2012. Kasparov retired from his chess career in 2005 and has since then concentrated on his writing and politics. In the 1990s Kasparov broke his ties with the FIDE and created his own organization and arranged his own World Championships. Simultaneously the FIDE arranged their World Championships, and for many years there was arguing about who was the true World Champion.

14. Vladimir Kramnik, Russia, World Champion 2000–2007

Kramnik became World Champion after he beat Kasparov in 2000. In addition to having won three World Championships, he has also won the Chess Olympiad three times, together with the Russian team.

15. Viswanathan Anand, India, World Champion 2007–2013

Viswanathan Anand became a World Champion in 2007 and kept his title until 2013. Anand is Indian and very popular in his home country, where he has received an award for being the athlete of the century. Anand is also known for his interest in astronomy. When he is not playing chess, he likes to watch the stars from his telescope. His nickname is "The Tiger of Madras." Madras is the former name of Chennai, the city where Anand met Magnus Carlsen in the World Championship final in 2013. No one knows for sure why he is called a tiger, but it might be because he appears to be a mild and sympathetic creature but quickly turns into a dangerous predator when he sits down at a chessboard.

16. Magnus Carlsen, Norway, World Champion 2013

November 22, 2013, Norway's population erupted into cheers when their chess king, Magnus Carlsen, became a World Champion. The victory created chess hysteria in the country. Close to one hundred hours of chess were screened on TV. Schools cancelled their classes so their students could watch the chess games, and employers joked about implementing chess moves into their employees' salaries since they spent most of their time at work watching Magnus instead of working. Magnus became a Grandmaster at the age of thirteen. At that time he was the youngest Grandmaster of all time. Here are some of Magnus's many accomplishments:

- he is the World Champion in long chess and blitz chess
- he is the youngest Norwegian to receive the Peer Gynt Prize
- he has the highest rating of all time
- he has received the Chess Oscar multiple times
- he was the winner of several super tournaments

FIDE World Champions

Anatolij Karpov, Russia 1993–1999
Aleksandr Khalifman, Russia 1999–2000
Viswanathan Anand, India 2000–2002
Ruslan Ponomarjov, Ukraine 2002–2004
Rustam Kasimdzhanov, Uzbekistan 2004–2005
Veselin Topalov, Bulgaria 2005–2006

> Did you know that Mikhail Tal only had three fingers on his right hand? He was suffering from Lobster Claw Syndrome, a congenital condition that leads to a lack of fingers or toes, and that makes the hand or foot look not unlike a lobster claw.

The Weirdest Final

In 1978, Anatolij Karpov met Viktor Kortsjnoj, who was known by the nickname "Viktor the Gruesome," in what perhaps is the weirdest World Championship final in history. The final has been immortalized in *Chess*, the musical. During the match, Kortsjnoj was certain he was playing against the entire Soviet regime and that Karpov and his helpers were using dirty tricks, such as placing a parapsychologist in the room. Kortsjnoj responded by placing an anti-parapsychologist in the room so that he could hypnotize Karpov's man, and he played all of the matches wearing sunglasses. During the match, the famous "Yogurt Fight" also took place. In the second round, Karpov got delivered a yogurt. Kortsjnoj and his support team decided that the yogurt contained a coded message and they registered an official complaint. Karpov eventually won the match.

The Longest World Championship Match

The World Championship match between Anatolij Karpov and Garri Kasparov in 1984 lasted for 48 games! The first player to win six games would win the match, and many people though the match would be short as Karpov started with a 4–0 lead. But they were very wrong! After 17 remises in a row, Karpov won another game. With a 5–0 lead, the match should end soon? Four remises in a row were played before Kasparov finally won a game. Karpov was getting tired of the long match, and Kasparov won two games in a row. It was now 5–3 to Karpov, and the match was interrupted by Florencio Campomanes, the FIDE president at the time, because of a concern for the chess players' health. For instance, Karpov had lost approximately 20 pounds since the match started. The match continued a few months later, and Kasparov won at only 22 years old.

Restroom Fight

In 2006, Kramnik and Bulgarian Veselin Topalov met for a duel. Topalov caused a scandal when he accused Kramnik of cheating. Kramnik has a chronic disease and had to use the restroom 50 times during one of the games. Topalov suggested that Kramnik was hiding a computer in the restroom, and filed a protest. After massive quarrel and replay, Kramnik got to keep his title.

Smart Opening Moves

Earlier in this book you learned a few things about tactics. Now it is time for you to learn about strategy and what is smart to do in the different phases of a game. In chess, strategy is long-term planning.

We divide a game of chess into the opening, middle game, and end game.

The first moves in a game are what we call the opening. These moves may be very important for the rest of the game. Here are a few tips for the opening.

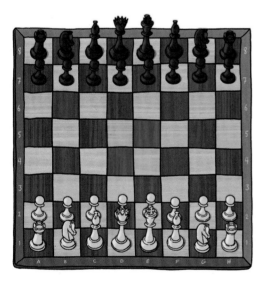

Fight for the Center

In the opening, it is smart to try and get control of the center of the chessboard.

The center is the four squares in the middle of the board.

Chess Custom 1
Did you know that you always have to shake your opponent's hand and greet them before you start a chess game?

Did you know that there are 400 possible positions after white and black have made a move each?

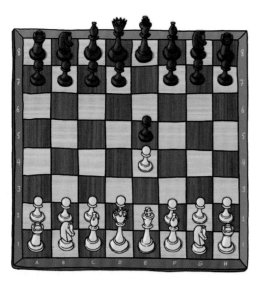

The pawns are good at controlling the middle. Therefore it's smart to move one of the pawns in the middle two steps in your first move. The pawns should be used to cover terrain, so that the officers can get the good spots. Together, the pawns create a skeleton on the board.

Both white and black have moved a pawn to the center.

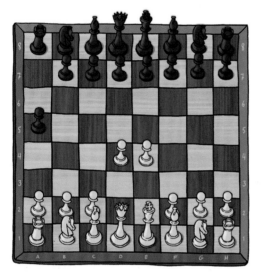

If you have the opportunity to move two pawns to the center, it can be smart to do so.

White has moved two pawns to the center, while black has moved a pawn to the edge of the board.

There's a saying: "A knight on the brink is a knight in the sand." It means that the knight is best placed when it is pointing toward the center.

Fast Development of Officers

In the opening, it is smart to move the officers out as quickly as possible. We call the knights and the bishops light officers, and the queen and rooks heavy officers. The light officers should move first.

When an officer is moved out of its starting position, we say that it is developing.

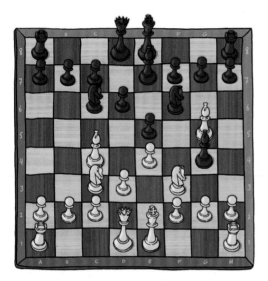

All the light officers are developed, and now the rest of the pieces can follow.

It is smart to develop officers so that they point toward the center.

Officers in the middle threaten several squares at once, while those on the edge are more limited.

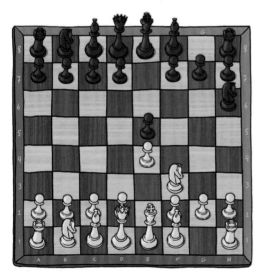

White has developed the knight so that it is pointing toward the center. Black has moved the knight to the outermost row, which we call the brink. The knight has short legs and does not like to be on the brink. Here the options are limited.

Did you know that the knight is the only officer that can move before the pawns have moved?

GRANDMASTER TIP
It is often smart to develop the officers on the king's side first, so that the king has the opportunity to castle.

PETER SVIDLER, RUSSIA

GRANDMASTER TIP

Fighting for the center and quick development are very important in the opening. That is what it is all about, even for the best players. Make the pieces cooperate and have them point toward the middle.

SIMEN AGDESTEIN, NORWAY

Get the King to Safety!

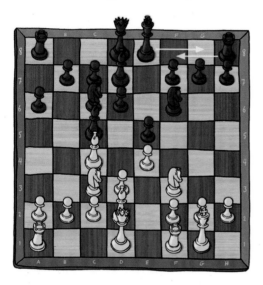

You can quickly get the king into safety by castling.

The light officers are developed. White has just castled. Black should do the same now.

Don't Waste Time Moving the Same Piece Multiple Times

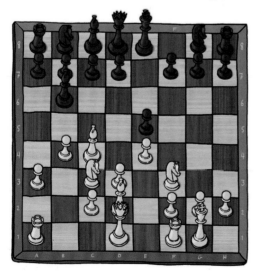

Try to avoid moving the same piece multiple times in the opening. Imagine your pieces are invited to a huge party. Everyone wants to go! Nobody wants to be left home alone. If a piece is left at the start, it won't be useful.

White has managed to develop all of its light officers in addition to placing the king into safety. Black has only moved the black bishop around. White is ready to attack with the entire army, while black is lacking its defense.

Don't Block the Way for Your Own Pieces

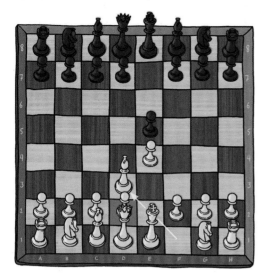

The pieces are a team. To win in chess, you have to get your pieces to cooperate. Avoid blocking the way for your own pieces.

The white bishop just moved to d3. It is now blocking the way for the pawn standing on d2. When the pawn on d2 is unable to move, the bishop on c1 is unable to move as well. It would have been much better to move the bishop to c4. On c4 it is both threatening a square in the center and it is not blocking the D pawn.

GRANDMASTER TIP
Do not cross the middle row before you have developed all of your officers. In the opening, it is a good strategy to move every officer only once. Chess was originally a game of war, and as a commander, it is logical to wait for an attack until all of your pieces are mobilized.
LEIF ERLEND JOHANNESSEN, NORWAY

Wait to Use Your Queen

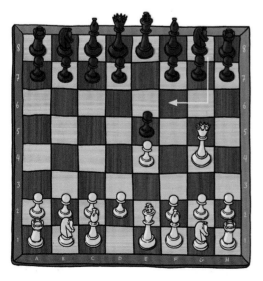

The queen is the strongest piece. It is therefore smart to wait to move her out until all of your other pieces are developed, and it is safer for her.

White has moved its queen out early. Black can now develop its knight in a square where it will be threatening the white queen. While white now has to use another move to move the queen, black can develop another piece.

Disrupt Your Opponent

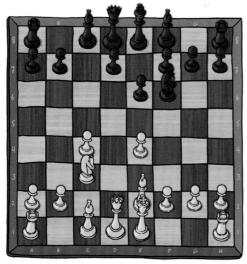

In addition to developing your officers quickly, you should also look for opportunities to disrupt your opponent's development.

Black has only developed one officer. Do you see what white can do so that the black knight will have to move back to the starting point?

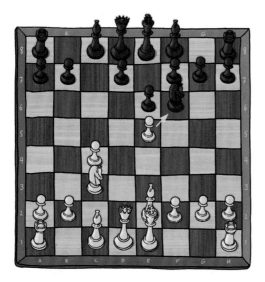

White can play e5. The pawn is now threatening the black knight. The only square safe for the knight to move to is back to g8 where it started.

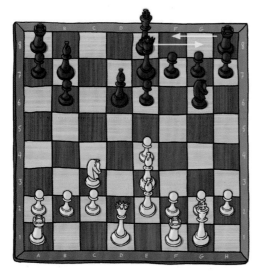

Black has developed all its light officers and wishes to castle in the next move to protect its king.

White can destroy black's plans. Do you see how?

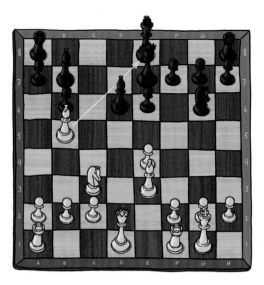

White can move the bishop to b5 and threaten the black king. If black is blocking the king with a piece, the white bishop will capture it. Instead, black needs to move the king. Now that the king has been moves, black cannot castle.

During the opening, your goals are to:
• get as many pieces as you can into play quickly
• gain control of the center
• place the king in safety

Simultaneously, you should try to prevent your opponent from doing the same.

CHESS CHECK 33

What do we call the beginning of a game of chess?

A) A warm-up

B) Castling

C) The opening

CHESS CHECK 34

In the beginning it is smart to...?

A) ...let the officers stay at the starting point

B) ...develop officers

C) ...move the queen out as quickly as possible

CHESS CHECK 35

In the opening it is important to put the king...?

A) ...in the middle of the board

B) ...into play

C) ...into safety

(Answer Key p. 167)

Common Chess Openings

Now you have learned several smart opening tips. With these tips you can now play the opening in multiple ways. There are some famous openings that are good to know. Many chess openings have been named after countries. Among others, there are:

- Italian   1. e4 e5, 2. Nf3 Nc6, 3. Bc4
- French   1. e4 e6, 2. d4 d5
- Spanish   1. e4 e5, 2. Nf3 Nc6, 3. Bb5
- English   1. c4
- Russian   1. e4 e5, 2. Nf3 Nf6

Remember that move 1 is both black's and white's first move. These examples are good ways to start chess games. Even though it is good to know these openings, the most important thing is to follow the tips that you have learned. Once you have played over these moves in different openings, there are several ways to continue the game. Many chess players spend a lot of time studying opening theory. But because there are so many ways to play the opening, it is almost impossible to learn them all. Some of the openings have funny names. Several openings have been named after animals. There are the Dragon, Hippo, Pelican, Hedgehog, and Orangutan, to name a few.

The weirdest chess opening name is probably the Frankenstein-Dracula Variation. Yikes! This opening is so crazy that we advise you not to play it. The moves are as follows: 1. e4 e5, 2. Nc3 Nf6, 3. Bc4 Nxe4, 4. Qh5 Nd6, 5. Bb3 Nc6, 6. Nb5 g6, 7. Qf3 f5, 8. Qd5 Qf6, 9. Nxc7+ Kd8, 10. Nxa8.

A Chess Opening Is Born

You met the humorous Dr. Savielly Tartakower earlier in this book, a man who was among the world's best chess players before World War II. According to him, something very special took place one time he visited a zoo during a tournament in New York in 1924. As he passed a cage with an orangutan, Susan the orangutan whistled after him. The Grandmaster got closer to the cage, and Susan did likewise. Tartakower picked his mini-chessboard out of his pocket and asked Susan if she had any chess tips for him. Susan took Tartakower by surprise and pulled him toward her and whispered in his ear "1. b4." The next day Tartakower surprised his opponent by following Susan's tip. Tartakower explained that the move b4 followed by b5 reminded him of the orangutan's moving pattern! And so the opening got the name the Orangutan.

A Smart Opening Trap

The Russian Trap

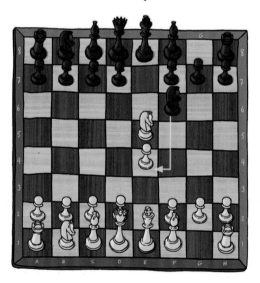

The Russian opening begins with the moves
1. e4 e5, 2. Nf6, 3. Nxe5

It is black's turn. Black can capture the
pawn on e4, but should watch out for the
Russian trap.

If black moves to e4, you can move the queen to e2. The queen is now threatening the black knight.

Do you see what smart move you can do after black has moved the knight?

You can move the knight to c6 and make a discovered attack with check. The queen is threatening the black king, and the knight is threatening the black queen. No matter what black decides to do, you can still capture the black queen with your knight. Black has walked into the Russian trap.

What went wrong? Let us rewind a few moves, to make sure you don't end up in the same trap.

Moving the knight to f6 was a blunder. Black should have instead moved its queen to e7 or played d6. If black plays Qe7 and white moves its knight to e4, black will win the knight back with the move d6.

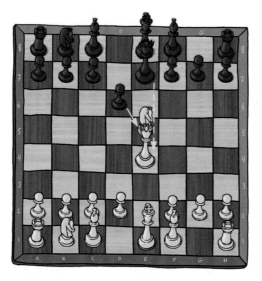

The knight is pinned and should not move because black will then capture the white queen.

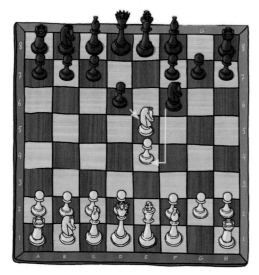

Rewind even further back.

After white captured the pawn on e5, black could have played d6 and threatened the knight away. Once the white knight has moved, black can capture the pawn on e4 with its knight.

Chess in Space

June 9, 1970, a historical team match took place. While one team was sitting in Russia, the other team was sitting in a spaceship that orbited around earth. In the match called "Earth vs. Space," the astronauts Nikolajev and Sebastjanov played against general Komanin and pilot Gorbatko. The game lasted for six hours and ended in a draw.

Did you know that in the old Soviet Union, simultaneous chess performances and blindfold chess were officially banned in the 1930s because they were considered harmful?

GRANDMASTER TIP

Chess is a lot more fun if you have a friend you can play against. You can practice together and learn from each other. And as you get better, you can travel to tournaments together as well.

ELISABETH PAEHTZ, GERMANY

Vulnerable Routes

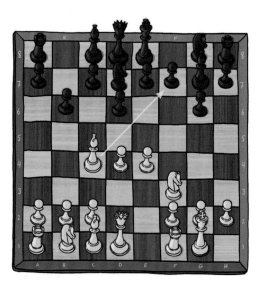

Remember that f7 is black's most vulnerable square before it has castled, and f2 is white's most vulnerable square. These squares are vulnerable because at the beginning of the game they are only protected by the king. Black moved the knight to d7 in its last move. That was not very smart, because now white moves the bishop to f7 and is threatening the king.

Black has to do something about the check.

If the king captures the bishop, there's a smart move white can make. Do you see it?

White can move its knight to g5. That is a check. The black king does not have many options for moves.

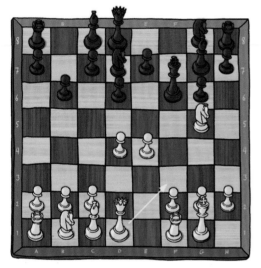

If the king moves to f6, the white queen can move to f3. That's a checkmate!

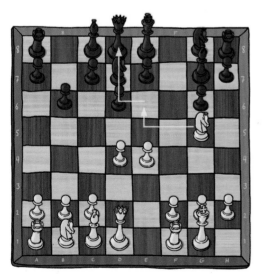

And if the king moves to e8 or f8, white can win the black queen.

White can move the knight to e6. The black queen is trapped. No matter what black decides to do, the white knight will capture the black queen in the next move.

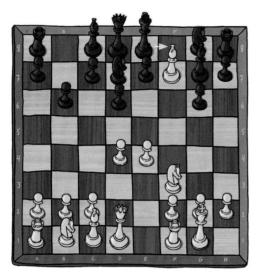

Let us rewind.

After white captured the bishop on f7, the best thing black could have done was to move its king to f8. But it would still not have been the best way to start the game, with the king exposed and no option of castling.

The Royal Game

Chess has been played by many royals. Some of them were strong players, others not so much.

Vilhelm Erobreren once broke the chessboard when he threw it at the head of a French prince after losing.

Prince Valdemar of Denmark played against King Knut the Fifth when they got attacked by a rivalry king. King Knut was killed in the attack, while Valdemar escaped by using the chessboard as a shield.

King Conchobar of Ireland was a man of priorities. He would divide his day into three halves: one third for drinking, one third for fighting, and one third for playing chess.

Chess: A Game of Skills

Chess is without a doubt a game of skills. It isn't possible to win by luck. In other games, a beginner can win over a more experienced player by just rolling the dice, or by picking the right cards. In chess, the result is affected by how you, as a commander, guide your pieces.

Did you know that in 1062 Pope Alexander II banned chess? Many people still continued to play, but they had to play in secrecy.

Smart Moves to Make in the Middle Game

The middle game is that part of a chess game that takes place between the opening and the end game. There is no clear line between the opening and the middle game, but for the sake of clarity, let's say the middle game starts when the development is complete and the king is safe. Here are some smart tips for the middle game.

The Officers' Wish List

- the king wishes to be safe
- the queen wishes to be as open a possible, with as many options as possible, so that she can participate in both the defense and the offense
- the rooks wish to stand in open lines, preferably in doubles (see the next page for an explanation of this)
- the bishops wish to stand in open diagonals
- the knights wish to occupy the front posts (see p. 139 for further explanation)

Keep the Pieces if You Have the Terrain

The pawns' locations often decide how much terrain, or room, the players have. In the diagram below, white has a terrain advantage because there are several white pawns occupying the black side. White should remain as it is. Black should try and spread out its pieces. If the pieces move, black will have more room for its pieces, and white will no longer have the advantage.

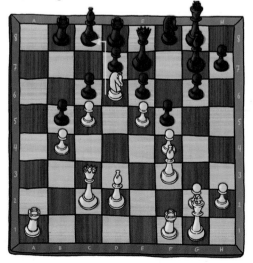

The white knight can capture the bishop on c8. Black will then capture the knight with one of the rooks. Even though the pieces carry the same value, this is a bad trade for white. Why? Because the white knight is very strong standing where it is. It is threatening many of the squares on the board and is controlling the black army. The black bishop on c8 is weak. It is almost blocked. It will take some time before it is able to improve its position.

The Rooks Enjoy Open Lines, Especially When They Can Work Together

The rooks are at their best when they are in open lines. An open line is a line with no pawns. A line with only one pawn is called a half-open line.

Doubling of the rooks can be a strong weapon, and they can become very dangerous on row. A doubling of the rooks means that they are placed on the same line or row.

Consider the same set-up in the last example. There is one open line on the board. Do you see which one?

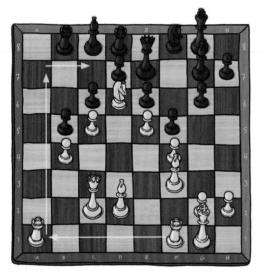

It is the A line. White should hurry to be the first one in taking control of the open line.

White has a plan to double the rooks on the seventh row by moving to the squares c7 and a7. Since white has a lot of space and black has limited space, white is able to go through with the plan without black stopping it.

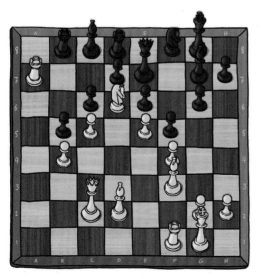

White moves its rook to a7. We know white's long-term plan, but this move will also open up the opportunity for a tactical trick for white. Do you see what white is threatening?

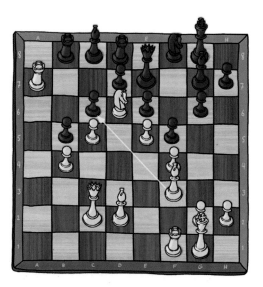

White is threatening the pawn on c6. Black cannot capture the bishop with its pawn on d7 because it is pinned.

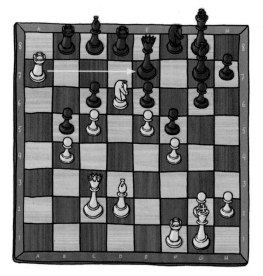

If the pawn captures the bishop, the white rook can capture the black queen.

When you have played a good game and your pieces are placed wisely, you are often rewarded with such tactical possibilities.

Attack if Your Opponent's King is Weak

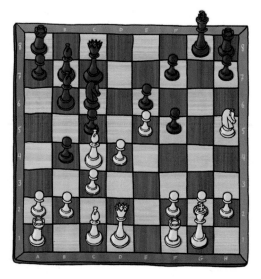

If your opponent's king is left unguarded, you should always look for possibilities for a king attack.

Black has forgotten to castle. The black king is misplaced and is vulnerable because the black B pawn is gone and so there is a half-open line toward the king. If the king makes it to the queen's side, he may be safe. White needs to act fast. Do you see what white should do?

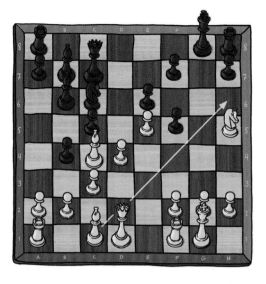

White should move its bishop to h6. The black king cannot move to f8 now and it is too late for a rescue.

White is threatening to move the knight to f6 and checkmate the king. In addition, the white queen is a short distance to the half-open G line.

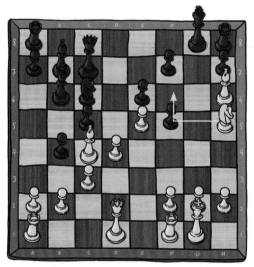

White was quick to take advantage of the weak position of the black king. If white had waited one move with the attack, black could have escaped. It's important to attack as soon as you have the opportunity.

A Deadly Battery

A bishop can become very strong as pieces are captured and the score opens up. With help from the queen, together they can make a deadly battery.

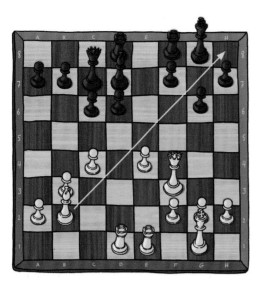

The white bishop on b2 is in control of the a1–h8 diagonal. Do you see what white can do to take advantage of this?

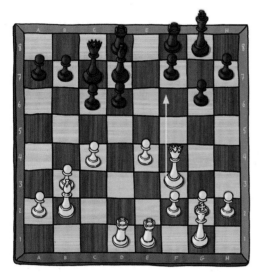

White can move its queen to f6.

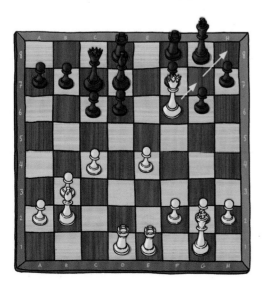

The queen and the bishop are now establishing a strong battery in this diagonal.

White is threatening the queen to move to g7 or h8. The black king cannot capture the queen because she is covered by the bishop. Black cannot stop the checkmate!

Don't Make Unnecessary Pawn Moves in Front of Your King

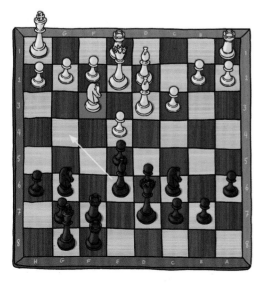

Since the pawns cannot move backward, you should think carefully before moving a pawn. This is particularly important when moving the pawns in front of the king.

It's white's move, and white is scared that black is going to play Bg4 in the next move. If he does so, the knight on f3 will be pinned. White moves to h3 to prevent the bishop from moving to g4.

The move h3 was an unnecessary and unwise pawn move. The black bishop and queen are pointing toward h3 as a point of attack, and they have been given the opportunity to attack white's king.

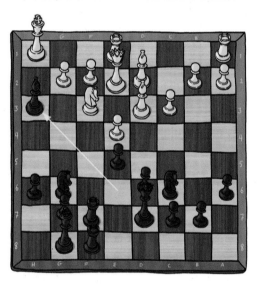

Black captures the pawn on h3 with its bishop.

If white retaliates on h3, the area around the white king will be wide open.

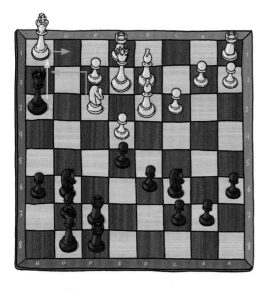

Black continues its attack and goes for h3 with the queen. The white king is now in trouble. White needs to stop the check either by moving the king to g1 or by moving the knight to h2. Will one of these moves save white?

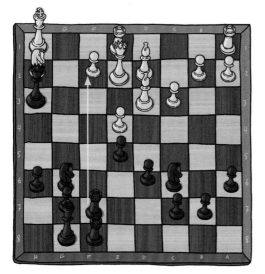

If the king moves to g1, black can capture the knight with the rook.

If the knight moves to h2, black can capture the pawn on f2 with the rook.

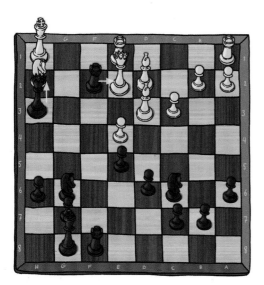

Black is now threatening with checkmate with its queen on h2, and the black rook is also threatening the white queen.

Imagine one small pawn move leading to all this mess for white. Always think carefully before you decide to move a pawn standing in front of your king.

If you've been paying attention, you might scratch your head at this point. Didn't Grandmaster Jan Gustafsson say it was smart to move a pawn in front of the king to avoid being trapped? And it's true, sometimes he is right. If your opponent is a direct threat, you should of course move a pawn to avoid being trapped. But in the previous example, it was not the smartest thing to do. There were no threats against the black king, and then it was unnecessary to move the pawn. Something that is a good idea in one game, might be unwise in another. There is no blueprint for playing chess. That's what makes the game so much fun!

GRANDMASTER TIP
When your opponent moves, try to understand their reason behind the move, and see which of your pieces might be threatened.

NIGEL SHORT, ENGLAND

GRANDMASTER TIP
For each move your opponent makes, it's good to ask yourself the question: "Why did he make that move?"

NILS GRANDELIUS, WWEDEN

Occupy the Front Posts

In the middle game you should try and place your pieces in a way that makes the pieces as active in the game as possible. A smart way to find good spots for your pieces is to look for front posts. A front post is a square that is located on the opponent's half of the board. It is covered by a pawn, and it cannot be threatened by the opponent's pawns. Look at this scenario:

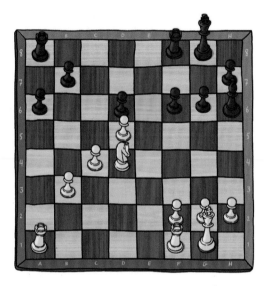

The square e7 is a front post for white. White can place its knight on e6. It can safely stand here and annoy the black pieces. Black cannot get rid of the knight without sacrificing a more valuable piece. The only way black can remove the knight is by capturing it with a rook.

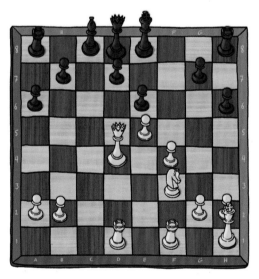

Here is a challenge. White has a front post. Do you see where?

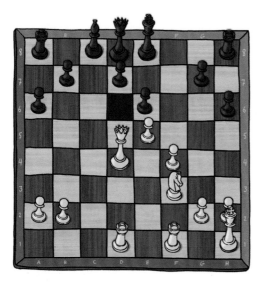

The square d6 is a front post. Do you see a white piece that would have liked to be in this square?

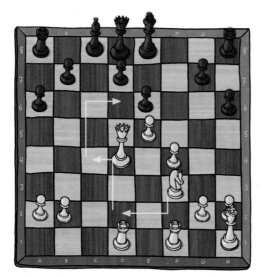

It is the knight. It needs to get there in three moves.

Knights can become very powerful in the middle game if they occupy a front post. A knight that has occupied a front post on the sixth or the seventh row is often as strong as a rook.

There are several different types of chessboards. If you are planning a trip, it is practical to have a small chessboard that can be folded. Folded chessboards were invented in 1125 by a chess-playing priest. At the time, the church was banning priests from playing chess. So he made his own chessboard that could be folded so that it looked like he was holding two books.

Beware Poisonous Pawns

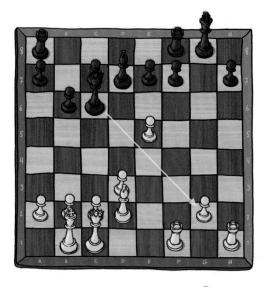

A poisonous pawn is a pawn that is uncovered, but still very dangerous to capture.

Black can capture the pawn on g2 with the queen, but this pawn is poisonous.

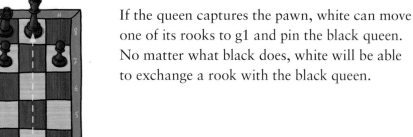

If the queen captures the pawn, white can move one of its rooks to g1 and pin the black queen. No matter what black does, white will be able to exchange a rook with the black queen.

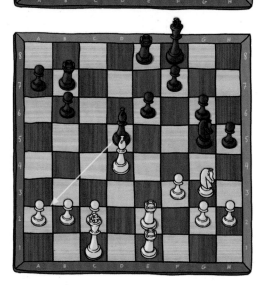

The black bishop is threatening the pawn on a2. This pawn is poisonous. Do you see why?

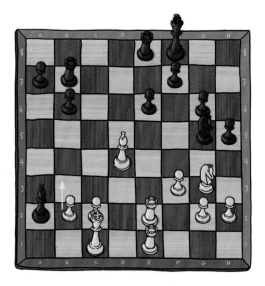

White can move the pawn to b3 and the black bishop will be trapped. The white king plans to move to b2 in the next move to threaten the bishop. For the bishop to move, it has to be exchanged with a pawn.

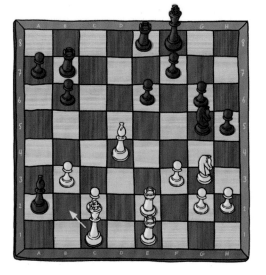

Black cannot prevent the bishop being trapped.

The Testament Pawn

Once upon a time there was an old man who did not have much time left to live. He wished for his son to inherit everything he owned, but he also wanted to make sure his son did not make the same mistake he did when he was playing chess. His son was to inherit everything he owned on one condition: that he never captured the pawn on b2 with the queen. This is how the pawn on b2 has gotten the name "The Testament Pawn." Today we use the same name on the pawns standing on b7, g7, and g2. These pawns can be poisonous.

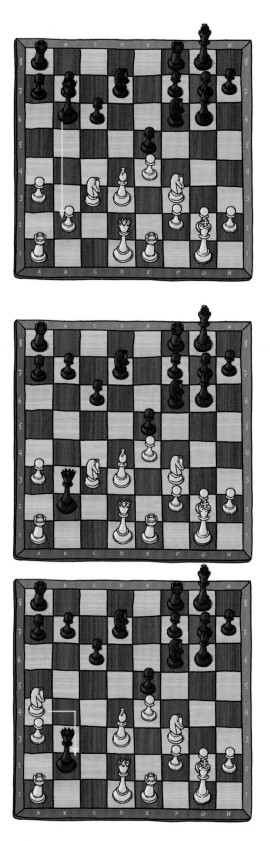

Here are some examples of how dangerous it can be to capture the pawn on b2.

Black is greedy and captures the testament pawn on b2 with the queen.

Black immediately regrets its greediness when white moves next. Do you see what white can do?

Na4!

The queen is trapped. No matter where the queen moves, she will be captured.

Whether the story about the testament pawn is true or not, we do not know, but it can at least remind you of how dangerous it is to capture these pawns.

Things to be aware of in the middle game:

- including all the pieces in the game
- looking for the best possible squares for the pieces
- avoiding making unnecessary pawn moves in front of your king
- attacking the opponent's king if it is poorly protected

GRANDMASTER TIP
Having control over the center is important in all phases of a chess game, not just in the opening. Pieces that are placed in or close to the center are threatening more squares than those pieces placed on the corners. Pieces that are placed in the center are very good as they quickly can join both defense and offense.
JON LUDVIG HAMMER, NORWAY

CHESS CHECK 36

Where do the rooks like to be placed the middle game?

A) Squeezed in a corner

B) They should be sacrificed in the middle game

C) In open lines

CHESS CHECK 37

What should you do with the king in the middle game?

A) Move it to the center

B) Move all the pawns in front of it, so it has a lot of space

C) Keep it safe

(Answer Key p. 167)

Smart Moves to Make in the End Game

When there aren't very many pieces left on the chessboard, you are playing the end game. In the opening and the middle game, it is all about keeping the king safe. In the end game, the king is a very important piece that needs to participate. Here are some smart tips for the end game.

Active Pieces

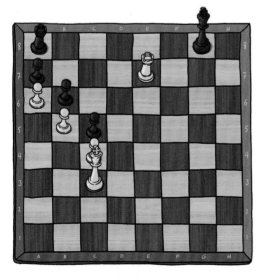

When you only have a few pieces left, it is important that they are as active as possible. An active piece is a piece that can easily move around on the board.

The white rook is very active. It can move to multiple places. The black rook is passive. Where it stands, it does nothing but protect a pawn.

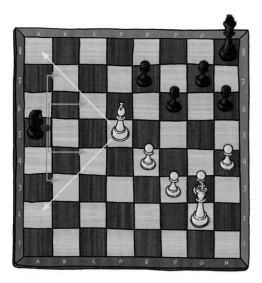

The players here are tied, but white's position is much better. Why? Because the white bishop is dominating the black knight. The knight cannot move because it will then be captured by the white bishop. The white bishop is very active, while the black knight is out of the game.

Bring in the King

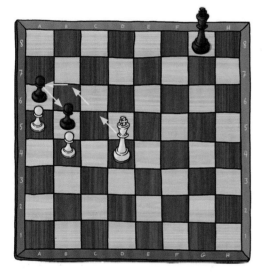

You have learned to protect the king during the opening and the middle game. In the end game, when there are only a few pieces left, it is important to bring the king into the game. The player who is the quickest to include the king in the game often wins the game.

The white king is approaching the black pawns. White is planning to capture them to create a free pathway to the last row for the white pawns. The black king is too far away, and he will not make it over in time to defend his pawns.

Try to Get a Passed Pawn

A passed pawn is a pawn which cannot be blocked by enemy pawns. A passed pawn can become dangerous if the opponent is unable to stop it.

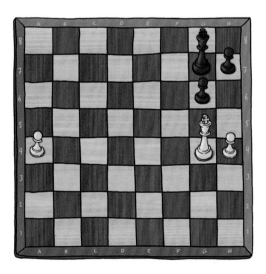

White has a passed pawn on a4. None of the black pieces can prevent it from reaching the other side where it can promote itself to a different, stronger piece.

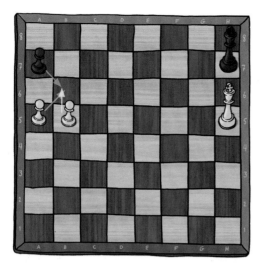

White is "making" a passed pawn by moving the pawn from b5 to b6. It is now threatening the pawn on a7. Black needs to capture the pawn so that the white pawn on a5 can get its revenge.

The pawn on b6 now has a clear passage to the other side. The black king is too far away to stop it.

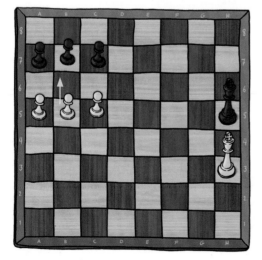

Sometimes it is smart to sacrifice a pawn to get another pawn to become a passed pawn.

The white pawns have come far, but the three black pawns are standing in their way. White has to be smart to get through black's pawn wall. White starts with b6.

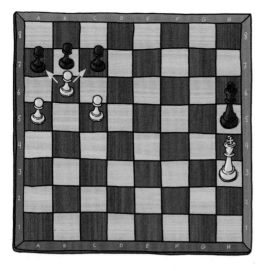

The pawn on b6 is now threatening the pawns on a7 and c7. If black does not capture the pawn on b6, it will capture one of the black pawns and in the next move it will reach the other side. Let us first take a look at what will happen if black captures with the A pawn.

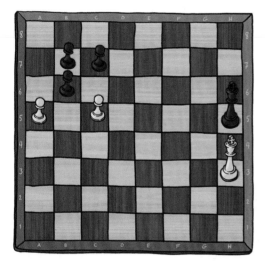

White can retaliate on b6, but has something better in mind. If the black pawn had not been placed on b7, the white pawn could have moved from a5 to a6, and then eventually to the other side. Because of this, we have to try and divert the pawn on b7. Do you see how?

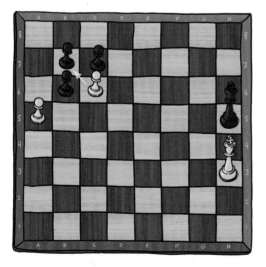

White is playing c6. The pawn is now threatening b7. The black pawn on b7 has to capture c6.

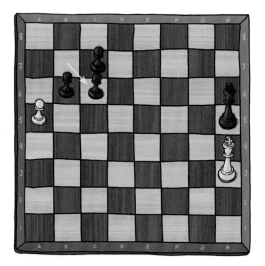

Do you see what white can do now?

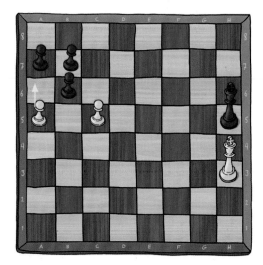

White can play a6! The A pawn is now unstoppable. White sacrificed two pawns to get a passed pawn. Even though black has three passed pawns, there is plenty to do before they all reach the other side. White can promote the pawn to a queen in two moves, and then capture the two black pawns.

If black had captured b6 with the C pawn instead, white could still have followed through with the same plan.

The pawn on b7 has yet to be diverted, but this time we should do it by moving the pawn on a5 to a6. If black captures a6 now, the white C pawn is free to go to the other side.

The job is not done when you've gotten one passed pawn to the other side. You should also know how to checkmate with the new piece you promoted the pawn to. In most cases, it is the smartest to promote to a queen, because she is the strongest piece.

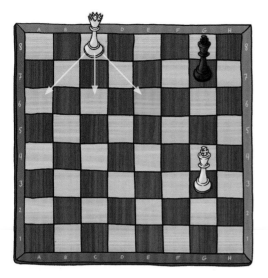

If you only have the queen and the king left, you have to get them to cooperate to checkmate. The queen cannot do this alone. She needs some help from the king. The black king can only become mate when he is placed in one of the corners of the chessboard. The king is only one row away from the eighth row, so choose to mate here. White has to make sure the black king does not come any closer to the center of the board, and so moves the queen to the row in front of the black king. The queen can move to a6, c6, or e6. Since e6 is closest to the black king, move her there.

The queen is now in control of the entire sixth row, and the black king has only a few options of squares he can move to.

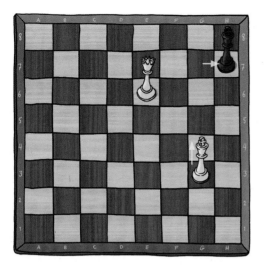

The black king moves to h7.

The queen remains where she is. White needs to get its king closer to the black king and moves to g4.

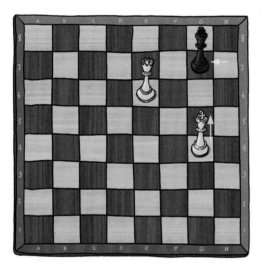

The black king stays in the seventh row. The white king moves one step closer.

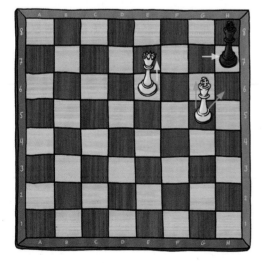

The black king moves back to h7.

The queen can now move one row up, to d7, e7, or f7, and threaten the black king. The black king is now unable to move to both g6 and h6, because the white king is threatening both of these squares, and the king is forced to move to the last row. Right where white wanted him!

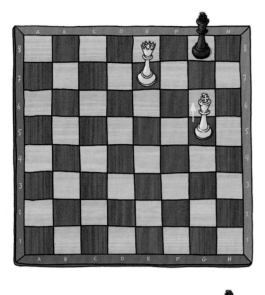

The queen remains in her place. The white king needs to get one square closer to the black king to block all possible escape routes.

The black king is squeezed in a corner, and the white queen can checkmate in five different ways.

It is not absolutely necessary for the king to be placed in a corner to create a mate. The queen can move to b4. The black king cannot capture the queen because she is covered by the white king. That is a checkmate!

Stop Your Opponent's Passed Pawns

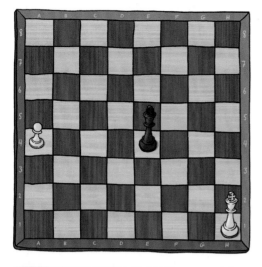

If your opponent has a passed pawn, you should try and stop it before it reaches the other side.

White has a passed pawn. It must be stopped!

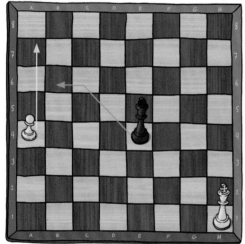

The black king is approaching the white pawn. The king will get closer by moving diagonally.

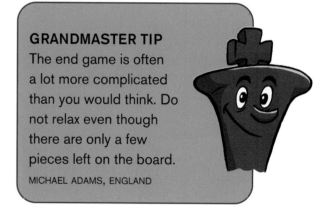

GRANDMASTER TIP
The end game is often a lot more complicated than you would think. Do not relax even though there are only a few pieces left on the board.
MICHAEL ADAMS, ENGLAND

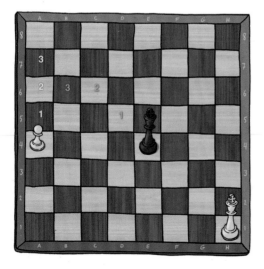

With three moves the black king can capture the pawn.

The white pawn is trying to escape, but the black king is catching up with it.

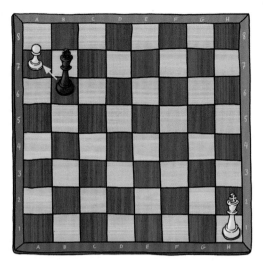

The white pawn is one step away from the other side, but black is on the move. Black captures the white pawn, and its fairy tale is over.

The Square Rule

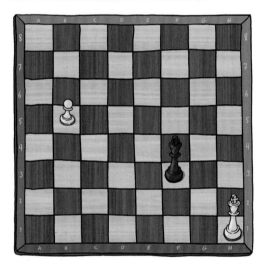

There is a way you can quickly find out whether a king will be able to stop a passed pawn or not.

The white pawn is approaching the other side, but will the black king catch it in time?

Make a square from where the pawn is placed. If the black king is standing within the square, or can get inside it within the next move, it will be able to capture the pawn. Will the black king make it? No, it is too far away. The white pawn is too quick for the black king.

Did you know that a square is a plane figure with four equal straight sides? A chessboard has the shape of a square.

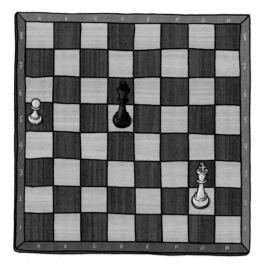

It is white's move. Will the pawn get to the other side in time before the black king catches it?

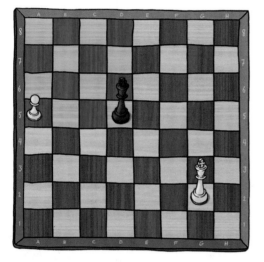

The black king is standing within the square and stops the white pawn.

The pawn is promoted to a queen, but her career is going to be short. Black captures the queen in the next move.

J'adoube

If you do not want to move, but only wish to correct one of your pieces that is not standing in the middle of the square, you may say "j'adoube" (pronounced Zha-DOOB). It is French and means "I adjust." You have to say this before you touch the piece.

Chess Joke

Two scientists, one of them sitting in the North Pole, the other in the South Pole, were playing correspondence chess. Every fourth month one of them would receive the other's move, which was delivered by a dogsled. The game had lasted for several years, and it was starting to get very exciting in the middle game. The scientist on the North Pole had the black pieces and was waiting in excitement for his opponent's next move. But four months passed by, and no letter came. After he had been waiting for nine months, he could finally hear the sled approaching. He was incredibly excited when he received the envelope containing white's move. Inside, all the letter said was, "J'adoube."

Zugzwang

Once in a while situations occur where you wish you could just say pass, and let the opponent move instead. It might be because you are in a so-called zugzwang. Zugzwang is a situation where a player must make a move, but making a move will put them at a disadvantage and they would much rather prefer to pass.

In this case neither white nor black wants to move. They are both in zugzwang. If it's black's move, he has to move the king to e7. That is the only legal move.

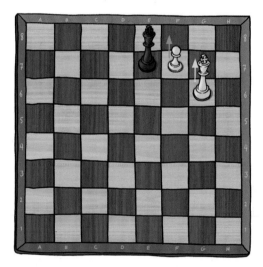

White can now move its king to g7. From there, the king is covering the square f8, and in the next move the pawn can move there and promote to a queen.

Why shouldn't you buy a house from a chess player? They spend too much time moving.

Chess Custom 2
Did you know that you always have to shake your opponent's hand and thank them for the game once it's over?

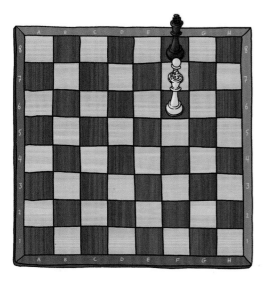

If it is white's turn instead, he must move his king to f6 to continue to protect the pawn on f7. It is now a draw! If white moves its king to another square than f6, black can capture the white pawn, and with only the kings left, the game is a draw.

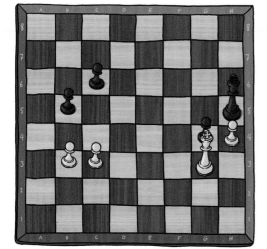

It's white's move.

Do you see how white can get black into zugzwang?

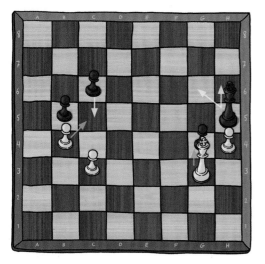

White is moving the pawn to b4! If black moves its king, the white king can capture the pawn on g4. If black moves its pawn to c6, it will be captured by white pawn on b4. No matter what black does, white will win a pawn.

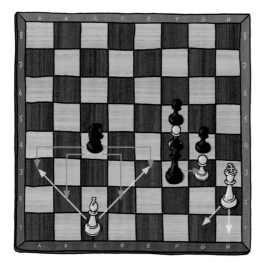

White is in zugzwang. No matter what white decides to do, it will lose a piece. If the king moves, the black king can capture the pawn on g3. If the bishop moves, it will be captured by the black knight.

In short, this is what you should do in the end game:

- get your pieces to be as active as possible
- include your king
- try to create passed pawns
- stop your opponent's passed pawns, if they have any

CHESS CHECK 38

What should the king do in the end game?

A) Play actively

B) Hide

C) Avoid moving

CHESS CHECK 39

The end game is all about...?

A) ...having as many pieces as possible

B) ...having active pieces

C) ...having passive pieces

CHESS CHECK 40

What should you do if you have a passed pawn?

A) Sacrifice it

B) Let it be

C) Try and get it over to the other side, so that it can be promoted into another piece

(Answer Key p. 167)

Can You Find the Master Moves?

These problems are a little bit trickier than those you have previously solved. But you are about to become a king of chess, so perhaps you'll be able to solve them. The answer key is on p. 170.

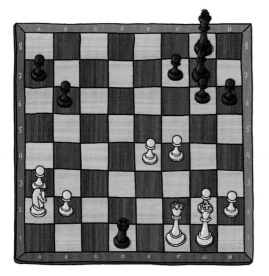

1. Ernst Grünfeld versus Aleksander Alekhin (1923)

Black's move.

How can black force a the corridor mate?

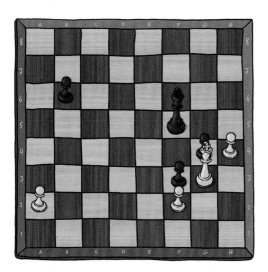

2. Ruslan Ponomarjov versus Vladimir Kramnik (2012)

White's move.

Can you get black into zugzwang?

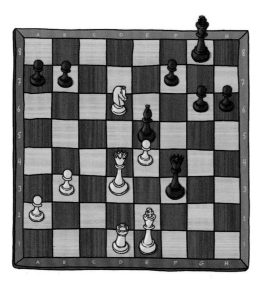

3. Sergej Movsesjan versus Vladimir Kramnik (2010)

Black's move.

Black won one of white's heavy officers. How?

4. Bobby Fischer versus Victor Ciocaltea (1962)

White's move.

Are you able to catch the black queen?

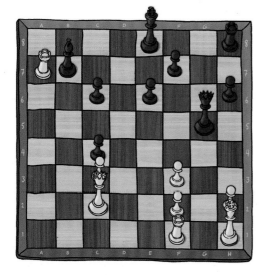

5. Ratmir Kholmov versus Mikhail Tal (1949)

Black's move.

Black did a diversion sacrifice and won white's strongest piece. How?

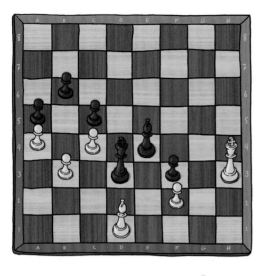

6. Viktor Sereda versus Tigran Petrosjan (1945)

Black's move.

Can you capture a piece?

7. Levon Aronian versus Magnus Carlsen (2010)

Black's move.

Magnus did a clever diversion sacrifice. Can you identify it?

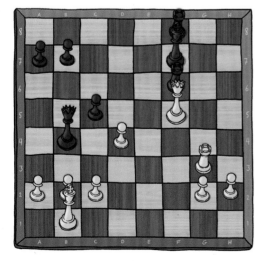

8. Magnus Carlsen versus Sipke Ernst (2005)

White's move.

Magnus sacrificed a rook in the last move. How can he now checkmate?

Fun Chess Variants

There are several fun variants of chess. Here are a few of them.

Bughouse Chess

In bughouse chess, four players play in teams of two. Partners sit next to each other and one player has black while the other has white. Normal chess rules apply, but captured pieces on one board are passed to the players of the other board, who then have the option of using those pieces on their board.

Relay Chess

In relay chess there are two teams. In addition to a chessboard, you need a game clock. The chessboard is placed at a distance from the players. The person who is going to move, has to run over to the chessboard. To make it extra fun, you can play with penalty laps, which means that whenever someone loses a piece they have to run as many laps as the piece that was captured was worth. If a pawn was captured, the team has to run one extra lap, and if a rook was captured, the team needs to run five loops.

Basket Chess

In basket chess you need a game clock and a can or a box. Each time a piece is captured, you have to try and throw the piece in the can or the box. If you miss, you must run as many penalty laps as the piece that was captured is worth.

Atomic Chess

Standard rules of chess apply, but if a piece is captured, all the other pieces next to it or diagonal from it are captured as well. The piece that captured it also disappears in the explosion. The king can also be blown to pieces, and whoever blows up the opponent's king wins.

Missile Chess

Standard rules of chess apply, but a player can make multiple moves in succession. White starts with one move, and then black can do two moves, and white can do three moves and so on. You need to have a good plan here! When one player checks their opponent's king, it is automatically the opponent's turn no matter how many moves are left. You have to checkmate to win.

Capture Chess

In capture chess you actually want to lose your pieces. If you are threatening one of your opponent's pieces, you have to capture them. The king can also be captured. Whoever is left with no pieces wins.

Hidden Queen

In this variant, both players have an extra queen dressed like a pawn. Both players decide themselves which pawn is to be the hidden queen and they write it down on a piece of paper. The pawn dressed as the queen can move like a queen whenever he wants. Like standard chess, you have to checkmate to win.

Blindfold Chess Record
November 26–27, 2011, the German player Marc Lang set a world record when he played blindfold chess against forty-six players at once! Lang won twenty-five games, had nineteen draws, and only lost two.

What's Next?

You have now learned a lot about chess, and maybe you even solved most of the problems in this book. Now it is time to play for real. Only by playing a lot of chess will you truly become an expert at chess!

You can play on a regular chessboard, or against a computer. It is also possible to play against other people online. Thousands of people are online and are waiting to play against just you. There are plenty of websites you can play on: chess.com, chessclub.com, and chess24.com.

There are also tons of chess apps, if you wish to play from your smartphone.

The very best thing to do is to play for a chess club. You will meet other players and have the chance to play against people your own age.

Best of luck in all of your future chess games! Hopefully we will see you in a chess club or in a chess tournament very soon.

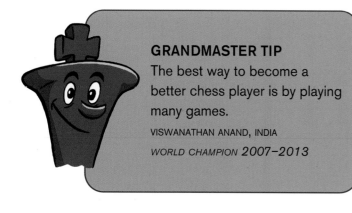

GRANDMASTER TIP
The best way to become a better chess player is by playing many games.
VISWANATHAN ANAND, INDIA
WORLD CHAMPION *2007–2013*

Answer Key

Chess Check

1: B	9: B	17: B	25: B	33: C
2: A	10: C	18: C	26: B	34: B
3: A	11: B	19: C	27: B	35: C
4: A	12: A	20: C	28: B	36: C
5: B	13: A	21: B	29: A	37: C
6: B	14: C	22: B	30: C	38: A
7: C	15: A	23: A	31: A	39: C
8: B	16: B	24:C	32: C	40: B

Do You Remember the Mates?

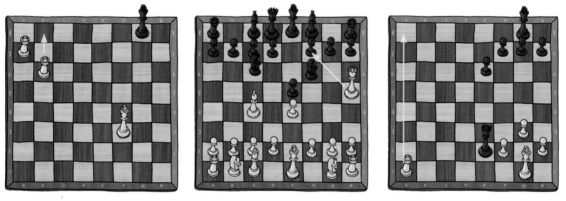

1: Rb8++   2: Qxf7++   3: Ra8++

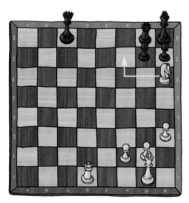

4: Nf7++

Can You Find the Mate?

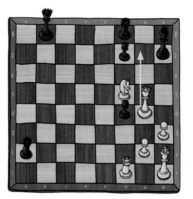

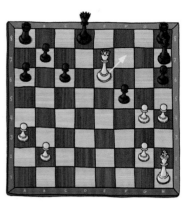

1: Rh8++

2: Qg7++

3: Qf7++

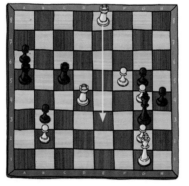

4: Rc2++

5: Rd3++

6: Qf3++

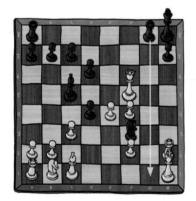

7: Rg1++

8: Qb4++

Are You a Tactical Master?

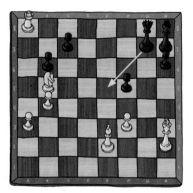

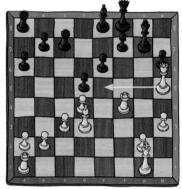

1: Qe5+

2: Qe5+

3: Nd2

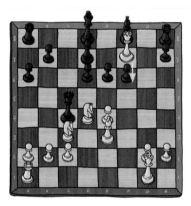

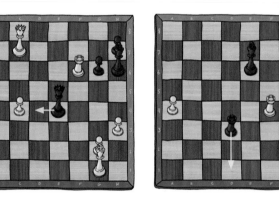

4: Qxf6+

5: Qd4+

6: Rd1

7: Bd3

8: Bg6+

9: Re5

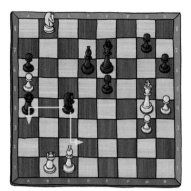

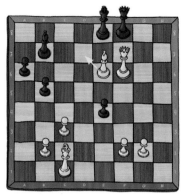

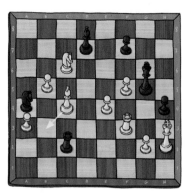

10: Nd2 eller Na3

11: Bd7+

12: Bb3

Can You Find the Master Moves?

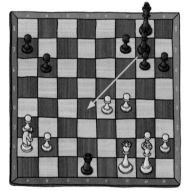

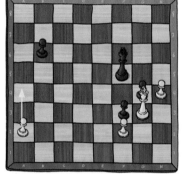

1: Bd4+

2: a4

3: Bc3+

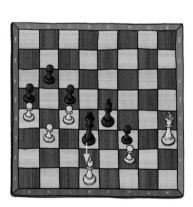

4: Bg5

5: Rg8

6: Kd2

7: Bxg2+   8: Qd7++

Thank You

Thank you Silje Bjerke, Ellen Øen Carlsen, Hans Olav Lahlum, Jan Gustafsson, Leif Erlend Johannessen, Maria Pitz Jacobsen, Jonathan Tisdall, Sheila Barth Sahl, Atle Grønn, and Anna Rudolph for all of your help, good advice, and contributions to this book. A special thanks to Silje Bjerke for her extraordinary work as a consultant.

Thank you Magnus Carlsen, Viswanathan Anand, Michael Adams, Peter Svidler, Nigel Short, Francisco Vallejo Pons, Jan Gustafsson, Jan Smeets, Jon Ludvig Hammer, Simen Agdestein, Sune Berg Hansen, Leif Erlend Johannessen, Pia Cramling, Nils Grandelius, and Elisabeth Paehtz for your brilliant Grandmaster tips.

Bibliography

Chess: From First Moves to Checkmate. Daniel King, 2000. Kingfisher Publications Plc
Kongenes spill-spillets konger. Knut Bøckman, 1996. Universitetsforlaget
Sjakk. Haakon M. Kibsgaard, 1984. Teknologisk forlag
Sjakkhåndbok. Anatolij Karpov, oversatt av Petter Svanevik, 1997.
Egmont Hjemmets Bokforlag
Sjakkmaskinens hemmelighet. En historisk roman. Robert Løhr 2008. Aschehoug
The Complete Chess Addict. Mike Fox and Richard James. 1987. Faber and Faber
VM Sjakk i 100 år. Portretter av 13 verdensmestre. Sigurd Heiestad og Øystein Brekke,
1986. Aventura Forlag

Internet

Tim Krabbé: Chess Curiosities

Wikipedia